## ABOUT THE

Nigel Barlow has made a living for many years speaking and consulting with the world's most famous companies, including Apple Education, BBC, Cigna, Danone, Lilly, Lexus, Microsoft, Nestlé, Hewlett Packard Printing, SKF, Standard Chartered Bank and Vodafone. He has also spoken to audiences in government, business schools, education and the public sector. He was a founding director of the Tom Peters Company in Europe and until recently an Associate Fellow at Oxford University's Saïd Business School. He currently runs his own speaking and consulting company.

Nigel's focus is on practical innovation, applying his methods to topics like changing mindsets, possibility thinking, the innovator's DNA, inventing the future, the customer's experience in the digital age, creative leadership and rocking up your presentation or pitch. He's foolhardy enough to prefer the dreaded after-lunch speaking spot.

Nigel lives with his family in Oxford, England and Heathrow Airport Departures lounge – a great deal of his assignments are international.

## Praise for Nigel's speaking

'Being able to capture and retain the interest of an audience is not an easy task. This is why attending a presentation from Nigel brings you to a different dimension where he captures your attention from the very first second and is able to keep that interest through a full hour, with a rhythm and energy we can all learn from.'

**David Belles**
**Inkjet Commercial Category Manager, Hewlett Packard**

'Nigel has a fantastic ability to use his vast knowledge and experience to make his presentations dynamic, engaging and fun through using many everyday examples which are relevant and adapted for the audience and the subject.'

**Tom Johnstone**
**Former President & CEO, AB SKF**

'From the moment Nigel steps on stage he challenges your prejudices, questions your perceptions and rocks your world with his high energy. Then he really gets started … Quirky and inspiring, he broadens your horizons whilst never losing the empathy which is necessary to bring you along with him so you learn to see things in a new way and act accordingly.'

**Nick Kirkland**
**CEO, CIO Connect**

'Over the years Nigel has become one of the most sought-after speakers. His mix of visions for the future, business trends and societal changes is unique, making you raise your eyebrows. Energetic and entertaining, he is surely one of the greatest and most effective speakers I know around the globe.'

**Dagmar O'Toole**
**Director of Global Operations, CSA Celebrity Speakers Ltd**

'Nigel's presentations are some of the most dynamic and engaging ones I've ever seen, and I've seen a lot of talks.'

**Britt-Marie Hesselback**
**Founder, SpeakersNet AB**

'Nigel is really one of the best executive education speakers I ever met. All of my clients who learned from him are impressed by his capacity to transmit, not only knowledge, but especially presentations that are exciting, compelling and memorable, which makes them ready to face future challenges. In a few words, he is able to transmit passion which helps you to win!'

**Giovanni Battista Vescovo**
**President and CEO, PromoStudio**

'Bringing Nigel on board of the New Time, New Way conference concept I had created for one of my clients has not only been the most relevant choice I could make but above all has resulted in the richest experience of content design I have ever had, in terms of added value, audience engagement and human relations, exceeding all expectations. He brought speakers and participants out of their comfort zone without them even noticing it, in a highly energizing and communicative way, with humour and style.'

**Suzanne Fellay**
**Strategic Communication Director, MCI Group**

'With speaking being the new rock'n'roll, Nigel engages his audience with every word and every gesture. His ability to keep hundreds of people rapt ensuring a lasting impression is an art; coupling this with outstanding content means Nigel's speeches live long in the memories for anyone who experiences them.'

**Nick Gold**
**MD and Chairman, Speakers' Corner**

# ROCK YOUR PRESENTATION

## NIGEL BARLOW

piatkus

PIATKUS

First published in Great Britain in 2016 by Piatkus
This paperback edition published in 2018 by Piatkus

A CIP catalogue record for this book
is available from the British Library.

ISBN 978-0-349-40890-3

Typeset in Palatino and The Sans by M Rules
Printed and bound in Great Britain by
Clays Ltd, Elcograf S.p.A.

Papers used by Piatkus are from well-managed forests
and other responsible sources.

Piatkus
An imprint of
Little, Brown Book Group
Carmelite House
50 Victoria Embankment
London EC4Y 0DZ

An Hachette UK Company
www.hachette.co.uk

www.improvementzone.co.uk

To Ian Craig Taylor
for teaching me the meaning of friendship

# MANIFESTO

*Rock Your Presentation* will save your audience from:

- Boredom
- Being drowned by PowerPoint
- A sudden impulse to leave the room
- Losing the will to live

This unnecessary suffering is caused by presentations, lectures and pitches that are as mind-numbing as muzak.

As an antidote, *Rock Your Presentation* will show you how to make your messages really strike home. It will improve your ability to give any presentation or talk in a more engaging, passionate and memorable way.

# CONTENTS

About the author  i

Foreword  xiii

Introduction: Why 'Rock'?  1

**Part I. Making Your Material Rock**

1 YOUR THREE-MINUTE SONG  15
Use a novel structure to make your talk more
exciting, engaging and memorable

2 SET THE STAGE  46
Create a speaker's 'rider' – preparing your
environment and audience

3 THE POWER CHORDS OF SPEAKING  71
Write stories, word pictures and lyrics that
illuminate your message

## Part II. Rocking Your Audience

4   SOUND AND VISION – A Punk Guide to *Life* by
    PowerPoint                                          101
    Experience a vocal and visual tune-up that
    avoids death by PowerPoint

5   PERFORM                                             131
    Understand the physical side of stagecraft –
    using your passion and your imperfections

6   ROCK THE CROWD                                      158
    Create interaction, getting the listeners' voices
    and minds into the room

7   ROCK YOUR PITCH UP                                  180
    A top ten of essential methods to grab attention

## Part III. Achieving Mastery in Speaking

8   GET EXPERIENCED – Learning from the Masters         201
    Explore what it means to develop your craft as
    a speaker

9   THE ZEN OF PRESENTING                               220
    Tune in to your audience ...

    SLEEVE NOTES                                        230
    Coaching, books and resources

    Acknowledgements                                    235

    Index                                               237

# FOREWORD

In 1985 I attended my first rock concert. The band was Tears for Fears. It's an evening I can still vividly remember even thirty years later for the passion, excitement and emotion. Since that night I've sat through thousands of speeches and lectures and it's fair to say that very few of them have had the same effect on me.

This is why I'm delighted that Nigel Barlow has written *Rock Your Presentation*. It offers a much needed guide to tapping into the magic that is created when a great rock band struts their stuff on stage. No one rushes to buy tickets to enjoy a night with their favourite band with the fear and dread that they might be bored senseless. However, most of us fear jumping on a stage to perform almost as much as the prospect of sitting through a business presentation.

Nigel Barlow writes with the credibility and stamina of a man who has delivered hundreds of presentations around the world as well as having sat in the audience at just as many. He passionately believes that we can take the tools and techniques from musical performers and use them to make our own presentations more exciting. Furthermore, he has the track record to prove it.

As a speaker agent for over twenty years and as an organiser of over five hundred business events, I know there is a real need for this book. *Rock Your Presentation* offers a comprehensive guide which can help transform you from the karaoke singer of your company to the rock star. Nigel helps keep your feet on the ground by emphasising that whichever tools and tips you use it is essential that you always remember to be authentic and true to yourself.

If you've bought this book to improve your public speaking you've made a great choice. Nigel will show you how you can better your skills, but more crucially, he will show you how to be different. You've joined the Rock Your Presentation band and Nigel is your roadie.

Brendan Barns
Founder, London Business Forum
London, England
August 2015

# INTRODUCTION: WHY 'ROCK'?

Many of the ideas for this book came to me sitting in the audience during so-so presentations. What? You haven't experienced the same mind-drift at the back of a lecture theatre? Of course you have – the sudden desire to play a favourite app on the mobile, recalculate your monthly mortgage payments or continue a texting marathon with that attractive newcomer at work? We quickly learn the skill of pretending attention, while our minds are busy elsewhere.

*But like you, I'd rather be captivated by a speaker – fully engaged and learning something valuable for my work or insightful about life.*

Do you want your talks, lectures, pitches or conferences to be more stimulating, interactive, moving and memorable? Then you've found the right book. **You need no specialist knowledge or interest in music** to get inspiration and practical ideas to liven up your presentation, to make it 'rock'.

*Rock Your Presentation* is for everyone who has to present or pitch ideas and wants to make their message hit home in a more profound way. Speakers, business people, lecturers, teachers and professionals who have to present ideas or information to their colleagues are who I've had in mind while writing this book.

We all know how a tune can stir and shake our emotions

and change our mood – many are unforgettable. I'd like to show you how you can achieve the same effect in speaking by 'rocking up' your material, without sacrificing depth or quality of thinking. Even enhancing it.

We'll be using the word 'rock' in two ways. Firstly, in its everyday, street meaning – to excite, to stir emotions, to make more intense. Applied to speaking, this means taking risks, breaking down boundaries between you and the audience and bringing your material to life.

Secondly, there are the musical insights to help you speak better. The music I mean by 'rock' is any modern music that moves and touches you. In this sense, we could say that Thelonious Monk, Bob Marley, Vanessa Mae, Eminem and Mumford & Sons all 'rock' – though you'd never find them classified as such on iTunes.

We can learn a lot from the way music affects the emotions and apply this to livening up our own speeches. That's what I mean by rocking your presentation.

While this isn't a basic guide – I'm assuming you have some experience of speaking publicly – it's stuffed full of practical suggestions for improving the way you present ideas. And if you are a beginner, why not start here so you don't have to work with all that dull 'pop' advice.

## How the Book Works

A key part of my speaking brief is to wake people up and make them think, frequently after lunch (often described as 'the graveyard shift'). I can honestly say I've learned as much to help me achieve this by listening to great music and seeing it performed live as from observing other business speakers.

The insights, inspiration and practical methods I've learned from speaking professionally in over thirty different countries, from the USA to China, is what I want to share with you.

But in a new way, beyond the usual muzak of presentation skills advice, which mainly focuses on logic. The Rock Your Presentation approach is logic *plus* emotion.

Creativity is often triggered by use of analogy and metaphor to get you out of your head – your usual, rational head that is. Music is the creative analogy I'm using, though you'll find there are many occasions when the art of speaking and that of playing music overlap strongly anyway.

Steve Jobs remarked that creativity is 'just connecting things'. Here's a flavour of the creative connections we'll be exploring to help you give better talks:

- Great songs often have strong **opening bars** and **climaxes**. So what's the equivalent in planning a talk?

- Confident music performers know how to **get the crowd involved**. Do you?

- Memorable songs have a **strong chorus**. What's yours?

- **Key changes** alter the mood of the listener. How can you introduce this concept into your talks?

- **Going unplugged** gives the feel of authenticity and intimacy in a concert – and a presentation.

- **Call and response** helps the audience to respond and agree, emotionally as well as rationally.

I have shamelessly plundered the topics of song writing, structure and the art of performance on your behalf. I'll be giving you short cuts, practical experience from my own professional speaking and from great presenters I've seen and sometimes worked with. If you have half the fun reading that I've had writing, I'll feel I've accomplished something worthwhile.

Listening to the music I refer to is optional, but it can be more engaging emotionally. You can download most of the songs mentioned if you go to my website, www.nigelbarlow. com, and follow the links.

My speaking work aims to stimulate creativity, so along the way I'll also be injecting some methods to help you be a little more curious and innovative in your everyday life.


## What Do I Know

My field nowadays is mainly business education. I've been lucky enough to work across industry sectors with many of the world's leading organisations, so naturally I'll be drawing on that experience a lot.

I make my living from speaking, sometimes in bizarre settings – from a kick-boxing ring to a ship, a ski lodge, a beach, campsites, a yurt, palaces, business schools, classrooms and many a hotel ballroom with its de rigueur pillars. It might be an intimate coaching session with an executive team or a project group; often it's speaking at a conference with anything from fifty to three thousand people in the room.

From all these diverse situations, what I'm reminded of every time is the importance of *tailoring* your content and your style of delivery to different environments and audiences to achieve different outcomes. I'll be giving you common-sense and creative tips to make it more likely that you also tune in better to your listeners.

I do know that I hate it when I'm labelled a 'motivational speaker', and can just about cope with being called 'inspirational'. That's because I believe I have stimulating and relevant content and insights – as well as a lively style. You need both.

Don't get the impression that it's always been a resounding success. When I look back on my early efforts I'm frankly embarrassed. Imposter Syndrome is a great way of describing what most of us have experienced. It's the awareness that we don't know as much as others think we do, accompanied by the uneasy feeling that we're about to be found out! Anyone suddenly promoted to a more demanding job, or having to speak about a topic they're not at home with, has felt a little of what it's like to be an imposter.

What I *don't* know is how well you, the reader, will learn practically useful stuff from a book as compared to face-to-face coaching. When I'm reading a book that aims to improve my skills, I'm the audience from hell. I just want to cut to the chase and get three or four good – and maybe one great – idea out of it.

That's why I've tried to present the ideas simply, clearly and free from jargon. And to make each chapter almost a stand-alone, so you can dive in where you like. For instance, you may want to make your existing talk livelier, or work on presenting it more convincingly – Chapter One, *Your Three-Minute Song* and Chapter Five, *Perform*, respectively would fit the bill here.

## You Cannot Be Serious!

'You cannot be serious!' was the response of an intellectual colleague when I told him about *RYP*. Wouldn't this be a triumph of style over substance, of showmanship over solid content, dumbing down for the age of attention deficit?

Well, you might think that a middle-aged man talking about rock is indicative of crisis. You wake up one day – many years too late – to realise that you'll never be picked for England, headline Glastonbury, appear in the Sunday Times Rich List or date a former Miss World. That's me. So now you want to *write* about music as a last attempt at being vaguely cool?

That's mostly accurate! Except I am serious about the practicality and usefulness of the ideas in *RYP*: they are all ones that I've seen used, or used myself to good effect. Well, nearly all. Some I've read about. But most of the research is experiential: giving presentations myself, listening to many more, reflecting, talking with lecturers, students, teachers, speaking agencies, conference production teams, innovative educators and ... you get the idea.

'Field' research is the usual label for this approach, except it was more like 'our man in the back row behind the pillar' research. (It's surprising that security doesn't move me on more often.)

The tongue-in-cheek part is because taking yourself too seriously will stop you connecting with anyone. Not taking the lecture or the audience seriously, however, is a sin. It's good to have a sense of the ridiculous: for the musician, that plucking a few strings is also going to pluck some hearts, for the speaker the notion that a hundred people will cease their conversation to listen to a complete stranger, for an hour or more. Achieving this requires an almost alchemical approach, where the audience is held in a state of suspended disbelief.

As well as covering ways of thinking more deeply about the craft of presenting, I hope to keep you entertained. I've given up reading many a book on this subject, and although there's no guarantee you won't quit *RYP*, I've done my best to make the ideas clear, accessible, insightful and fun.

My reply to the 'you cannot be serious' line is that I've often seen great material undermined, or even murdered, by meandering structure and dull delivery, even when given by some of the most brilliant thinkers. Simple does not have to mean superficial and a riveting performance can be used for even the weightiest of topics. I love the tale of an uneducated but smart woman, who said the person she'd most like to listen to was Albert Einstein because he spoke in simple terms that anyone could understand.

Popular music similarly speaks in an immediate and emotional language that anyone can grasp. The well-written three-minute song compresses more data – a whole story and emotions – into a small sliver of time than most means of communication. If you want your talk to be more engaging and enjoyable, there's a great deal to learn and apply from the art of writing and performing music.

Jiving like Jagger or crowd-surfing like Iggy Pop isn't the aim, and I don't expect your people to be singing hallelujah and waving their mobile phones in the air as you unveil the details of the new integrated supply chain strategy. But I do expect you to be able to keep them awake more effectively.

So why 'rock'? My serious friend said, 'Why don't you use opera?' Well, I could have used another musical form as a creative trigger, but making your presentations more classical, folky or techno doesn't convey the intensity of rock. Jazz it up? Maybe, though almost everything I've read on jazz applied to life centres around just one theme – improvise.

For the more serious-minded music listener, it's worth remembering that many of the great composers were strange and wild non-conformists. Classical musician and author James Rhodes* describes the great composers as the rock stars of their day – except he says that 'they didn't throw TV sets out of hotel windows – they threw themselves out!' Of Beethoven he observes:

> He was sullen, suspicious, touchy, incredibly messy and angry ... while every other composer was trying to woo their audience, he kicked down doors and planted bombs under their seats.†

There's no need for Beethoven to roll over – he's already rocking! New music from every generation challenges familiar formats, and steals from every genre. You have to do the same in speaking if you want to keep your listeners engaged. Forget for now rigid definitions of musical categories. Louis Armstrong has it right when he says: 'All music is folk music. I ain't never heard no horse sing a song!'

---

* Devoted only to the classics, he's becoming an iconoclast who is 'rocking up' his industry – while deepening the intensity of the listener.
† James Rhodes, *Instrumental* (2014).

*RYP* is about enhancing speaking from the viewpoint of music, so I've used examples you can directly apply to improve your own presentations. The songs I've chosen aren't necessarily my own favourite tunes and artists.

This has been hard! I'm a self-confessed music obsessive who listens to everything from sixteenth-century choral music to the very latest sounds. I know there are things in life more important than music: I just have trouble imagining what those things might be. I'm that annoying person who, in a restaurant or bar, filters out the conversation to tune in to whatever is playing in the background, like a human Shazam app.

Except for me, it's not merely background, rather it's life itself. Here I've attempted to control my passion for music because this is a book about speaking better, not music per se; the sounds take second place to the art of speaking. Doubtless you'll judge whether I've got the balance right.

## Pitches vs Presentations

Throughout *RYP*, I will use these expressions almost interchangeably, but there is a difference in emphasis. With a pitch, you are aiming to change someone's attitude and even behaviour, often looking for a resounding 'yes' to your idea or proposal. In presenting, you are primarily imparting knowledge and information, albeit as the seedbed for influencing thinking and changing minds.

Another difference is the context. You are unlikely to be purely 'pitching' to two hundred people: it's usually going to be a small group or even an individual you want to win over. You will see from the visual that it's a different starting point, but with considerable overlap. *RYP* applies to both scenarios, but I'll distinguish between the two approaches where it's useful to do so.

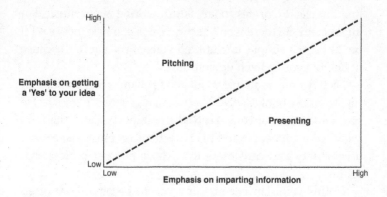

Like it or not, pitching an idea is something we probably all do several times a week without thinking of it that way, so it's a topic important enough to deserve its own chapter – Chapter 7, Rock Your Pitch Up. Charities, educational bodies and civil servants are constantly trying to 'sell' ideas as much as people in the world of commerce, even if they don't get so handsomely rewarded in financial terms.

As a good pitcher, you need to know how to present, while great presenters realise there's always an element of a pitch in what you do, whether you are updating people on the latest employee survey or trying to bring macroeconomics to life for a class of sleepy undergraduates.

What if you are constrained by having to deliver a fixed syllabus? Then work on what you *can* influence. You still have creative room to manoeuvre, focusing on how you structure your content, and how dynamically you convey it.

## The Passion of Amateurs

I can claim expertise in the art of speaking – although the moment you think you're an expert, you've stopped learning –

and am clearly 'professional'. But in writing about music, I'm an amateur. So there won't be any complex music theory – I'll be taking the simple, uncluttered view of the fan in the cause of helping you to liven up your talks.

Nick Hornby is an insightful and brilliant writer on popular music, whose book *High Fidelity* became a successful movie. He has, better than anyone, revived the importance of the fan's view – the amateur – and his reflections on music have more accessibility and directness than those of most professional critics.

In this vein, I'm encouraging you to become more of an 'amateur' in speaking. Sounds strange? It's less so when you consider the Latin root of the word: *amare*, to love. Amateurs fall in love with a subject and ooze enthusiasm about it. That's the short cut to connecting emotionally with an audience: show your passion. And you don't need to shout it out loud to be passionate – people will feel it if you can express it in your own, unique way. You have to be *both* a professional and an amateur.

There are numerous books out there exhorting you to become more professional in presenting material. *The Presentation Secrets of Steve Jobs* and *Talk Like TED* are two well-written examples, both by Carmine Gallo. But I'd rather you talked more like yourself. To be an authentic teacher, speaker or performer you need to find ways to simply be yourself. It's one of those clichés that persists because it's true.

Connecting with your own passion and choosing your unique way of expressing it is a theme that runs throughout *RYP*. More easily said than done, especially if you are nervous about speaking. How can you 'be yourself' in front of a hundred strangers?

I know you can – indeed *have* – to put your unique stamp on what you say, and *how* you say it. Not to be a 'cover version' of somebody else, but to be an original. That's what keeps listeners awake and helps you to come over as authentic. My nightmare scenario would be if you ended up presenting too much like another speaker you admire. My even darker dream would be to spawn people who presented like me! There's a wide enough range of ideas and tips in this book for you to cherry-pick and use the ones that work for you.

---

### On Being Yourself

I once read a piece of unexpected wisdom in an advertisement:
    Be yourself.
    You might as well –
    everyone else is taken!

---

I suggest that you read *RYP* interactively; there's a section at the end of each chapter that covers tips and ideas to improve your talk. There's also space for you to record the ideas that connect with your material. Scribble, mark and draw. Using the principle that 'real is best', immediately apply the ideas to a specific talk or pitch you are working on.

It's time to press *play*.

# PART I

# Making your material rock

# ONE

# YOUR THREE-MINUTE SONG – MAKE YOUR TALK MEMORABLE

- ◆ Short, Sweet and Tweet!
- ◆ Your Opening Bars
- ◆ Verse and Chorus
- ◆ The Bridge (or Middle Eight)
- ◆ Your Climax: Codas and Fades

Let's get straight into thinking about a creative structure and format for your talk. You are unlikely to be speaking for only three minutes – although it's worth remembering that the Gettysburg Address took only two and a half minutes – but the elements that make a rock song of that length so catchy, moving or unforgettable can be directly applied to create a strong framework for your own presentation.

A good three-minute song is a masterpiece of compression. Whole stories, emotions, characters and landscapes are grasped by the mind. Sometimes it's enough to hear only the first one or two notes of a familiar number for your brain to race ahead, chemically and electrically reproducing the rest. Often with remarkably high fidelity: your own built-in auto-tune.

Think how many years a song can lie dormant in your mind, only to be replayed mentally in full when you pass an open window and hear it playing. You might feel a warm and comfortable sense of nostalgia, or be annoyed because that was the artist your former partner used to like – and you never really got. Above all, it triggers memories, creates emotions and changes your mood.

By taking apart the structural parts of a powerful song, we can understand how to develop a more lively and memorable presentation. The building blocks of many successful tunes are:

Opening, verse, chorus, verse, chorus, bridge, chorus, fade or climax.

We'll explore how to use them to make your own talks more effective, after first extolling the virtues of 'the short version'.

◆

## Short, Sweet and Tweet!

Three minutes is ... short! The effectiveness of short songs tells us a lot about human attention spans: that they are ... short!

As a speaker or teacher, you're usually the one paying attention, while the audience may need jolting into a state where they are fully with you. Einstein once remarked that if you spend two hours with a beautiful woman, it seems like two minutes, but two minutes with your backside on a hot stove seems like two hours. That's relativity!

*The special relativity of speaking is that time for the listener and the speaker passes very differently.* It's rare for a speaker to just tune out, though not uncommon for dull delivery to switch the audience off.

Here are two ways to close the gap, to be more in rhythm with the listeners' perception of time.

Firstly, consider how much material – or how many slides –

you think you need. Then – cut 50 per cent out. That's right: 50 per cent.

My guess is you've still got too much.

When I've coached speakers for conferences, I've sometimes worn a T-shirt which says '50 per cent out', so the message is clear. Except that it limits me a bit when I have to say, 'Eighty per cent out, please.' Which is often. Don't just cut slides, but points and examples that don't add to your logic. Everything has to earn its place. Any doubt? Cut it out!

---

### Compressed Information (2' 41")

*New York Times* writer Neil Genzlinger was making a documentary about the 1960s. Influenced by Stephen Stills's famous protest song, 'For What It's Worth', he admitted:

'I have nothing to say that Stephen Stills didn't say better in 2 minutes, 41 seconds.'

'Looking Back on the Year That Sums Up the '60s',
Neil Genzlinger, *New York Times* (8 December 2007)

---

The second tip is: *the audience don't know what they haven't had.* They don't know what they don't know. So don't mention it! An over-diligent approach – 'they *have* to know this, this and this' – will mean you cover the material, but can't dive into it. It's too much for the listener; by 'covering' everything you're ensuring they don't retain much. It's like the history teacher who remarked, 'I taught them history, but they didn't learn it.' However, I bet he covered the syllabus.

The three-minute song that hits you through the airwaves and stays with you for ever is a lesson in concision. Try to get down the essence of your talk – you don't have to sing it. Note down and then dictate your main argument into the recording device you've got on your mobile. Do it in under three minutes.

You now have the basic message – everything else is example, detail and exposition.

## Even shorter ...

Peter Thiel, creator of PayPal and an expert on scientific and technical trends, remarked in 2014 that by now he'd have expected jet boots and *Star Trek*-style 'beaming up'. But what have we got? Twitter and its 280 characters! What Twitter *does* do well is focus us on brevity. When you can't put it over in tweet-size, you probably can't convey it coherently.

Here's my personal, preparatory tweet for a forty-minute talk on the topic of brands to 150 leaders of a Nordic engineering company:

> Why brand? Ubiquity-striptease. €€ of B2B brands: margins and stock price. Assess our brand perception – learn to live it.

Ninety-six characters. Don't worry, the talk was quite enough to fill up the time when I'd put in examples and stories! The 'striptease', by the way, was unveiling well-known logos gradually to see how quickly they were recognised. This led to a deeper conversation about how subliminal, pre-conscious and emotional a brand could be, segueing into a discussion on the relevance of this in the business to business space.

I don't think I'd have written 'striptease' in a longer note format, and yet it triggered a whole new line of thinking. I like the prompt at the end of a tweet when you've gone over the allotted number of characters: 'Be more creative.' It forces you to cut to the chase, in the same way that writing a short but incisive proposal or talk does.

Michael Frayn is a brilliant exponent of the short version – he's a master of short plays, sketches and skits.

'I have to say that I like short things,' Frayn reflects.

'Wittgenstein's *Tractatus Logico-Philosophicus* is very short. If he can give a complete account of the logic of the universe in 20,000 words, why does anyone need more for anything?'*

Why indeed? A sobering but valuable minor chord of an idea to make me and you reflect on whether we couldn't say it in less time, more clearly and with fewer words.

Now that you have the essence of what you are saying – it's a good start – let's borrow liberally from the elements of song structure to bring your material alive.

## Your Opening Bars

People remember starts and finishes – psychologists call this 'primacy' and 'recency'. The beginning of a movie and its climax stay in your mind, while there's a great deal of fidgeting during some of the middle passages. Think of the opening of *Raiders of the Lost Ark*, when Indiana Jones is nearly killed a dozen times in five minutes. Your attention is grabbed. Start strongly and memorably – like Led Zeppelin's 'Immigrant Song' – and you are on a roll.

It's the same with a talk. Begin uncertainly and you may always be out of step, with yourself and the audience.

Rehearse your beginning. I might do this out loud while driving to the venue. Try it several times. Your inner ear, whether musical or not, will *feel* where you are lacking enthusiasm and clarity, or just being boring.† Telling the listeners in some detail what you are going to be telling them, then telling them – all that old 'muzak' advice. You'll hear it in your voice as a dead note; it's boring and unconvincing, even to yourself.

Saying 'I'll come to that later' also creates a certain heavi-

* 'Michael Frayn: "I was in a very lucky generation"', *Daily Telegraph* (2 May 2015).
† I've sometimes played a snatch of the Pet Shop Boys' 'We Are Never Being Boring' as a jolt to speakers I'm coaching.

ness rather than anticipation in the room. Frankly, they don't give a damn – do come to it later rather than mention it. For the audience, there's only now, and you need to travel the journey *with* them.

So how do you start? You could try a little drama. Watch the opening of the Talking Heads' concert film, *Stop Making Sense*.

Lead singer David Byrne comes onto the stage alone with an acoustic guitar and deposits his cassette player on the stage. Dancing with his awkward leggy movements, he proceeds to play solo the uncomfortable yet beguiling strains of 'Psycho Killer'. It's hypnotic and striking. Above all, he's demonstrating his openness and vulnerability, and whether you like his performance or not, he is truly *there*. He's marked his presence in the room with you. In everyday terms, he's got your attention. And how!

## Silence is golden

Your 'opening bars' are unlikely to be so dramatic in a business or educational setting, so what can you do?

The counterintuitive answer is to start with **silence**. Four seconds will usually do it. Think of the collected stillness that settles on a room when the conductor is raising his baton in preparation to launch into the resonant opening notes of Beethoven's Fifth – one of the greatest riffs of all time – or the anticipatory silence when the members of a rock band come onto stage, pick up their guitars and look at each other before hitting that first note.

---

### Sufjan and Silence

Sufjan Stevens is an eccentric multi-instrumentalist. His 2015 album, *Carrie & Lowell*, is a masterpiece of using silence and pauses to deepen the intensity of emotion. Handle with care – a friend played it in the coffee shop he runs, only to find his clientele coming over all weepy. It's not surprising: it's about Stevens's grief at the death of his estranged mother. Sweet-sounding and sad at the same time, it's an object lesson in not needing to make a big sound to show your passion.

---

Music and speaking rely heavily on the balance between silence and sound. It's the spaces, or rests, that make the sound. The music I love the most is laced with silences that hum, silences between the notes, between voice and guitar, one passage and the next.

## Open with a provocation

Then what to say first? It could be a provocative statement, a long lingering note that will find its resolution later in your talk.

Recently in London I was asked to speak about the customer experience to 120 managers from different companies. The organiser gave me a throwaway comment half an hour before the start:

> Nigel, nobody cares about customers any more.

He was being ironic, but in today's online marketplace, where all is being reduced to a click and a transaction, he had a point. His challenge became my opening statement.

'Nobody cares about customers any more,' repeated twice, is obviously not a logical way to start a talk on the benefits of loving your customers to death, but it resonated. I was then able to explore how difficult it is to really understand *anyone's* problems in life, let alone that of someone 'out there' – the poor customer – especially in the digital world.

I returned to this phrase at the end, as a view to be challenged by everyone in the room.

Alternatively you could start with an **example or story** with a hook, preferably one that embodies your theme.

---

### The Opening Bars in a Pitch

In a pitch, a compelling opening is everything. The listener's brain is searching for reasons *not* to attend to what you're saying – they've already heard three presentations and they will only tune in if there's a change of pace, tone, image or sound. You can do this easily if you just put your attention on it. Gather up the silence and then launch in with a phrase, a number or a picture that brings them out of their imminent torpor.

What will accomplish this most, and make them care, is a statement or hook about *themselves*, individually or as an organisation. It could be a problem – 'you've lost control of your market' or 'your competitors are eating your lunch'. Then it's good to soften it a little with the benefits of this conversation – 'we believe we have a solution'.

It's amazing how many pitches start with twenty slides about the pitcher's *own* organisation, track record, a list of very clever people in their business, and *yawn, yawn, yawn*. If you were listening to this like a song on the radio, you would already have changed stations.

It's the same in a meeting room.

---

Inspirational educator Professor Bill Rankin works with Apple Education, pioneering innovative approaches to learning.

In Toronto, I saw him wow a crowd of several hundred top educational minds, beginning his talk with a 'Brief History of Interior Lighting'! Who says Americans don't do irony? Having announced his theme, he beams at the audience and says: 'I know you're all as thrilled about this as I am!'

He then proceeds to spend nearly five minutes, with powerful slides, detailing how the ratio of energy input to output in lighting homes has improved over the centuries, from candles to early electricity to LED lighting.

His point? There are several here, and he segues effortlessly into explaining how the amount of useful *output* from education doesn't relate to the *input* of energy, how much effort is wasted and why so much schooling is still in the candle stage, while there's the new electricity of technology all around.

Bill Rankin has performed a 'Psycho Killer' of a start. By using a short story or example that illuminates his main theme.

One health warning: Bill is a very experienced speaker, so only use this approach if your story or analogy is strong, has good links and above all you feel confident in delivering it.

However you achieve it, the DNA of your talk is in the opening bars. A thought-provoking question you are going to answer, a powerful story or a bold one-sentence summary. Think of it as a gripping trailer that signals the possibilities to come.


## Verse and Chorus

The striking openings we've been exploring contain the seeds of your chorus, the theme you're going to return to, writ large and boldly stated. And, like the early notes in a great symphony, or thunderous riff in a rock number, it will be repeated, echoed and explored. Your chorus is *the bit you don't want people to forget!*

Creativity and Copying is one theme I've been asked to speak about. To introduce it, I've tried a simple experiment with audiences. I play them a cover of a song they all know, in a version with the chorus omitted. It's singer Cat Power's take on the Rolling Stones' 'Satisfaction'. She's left out the chorus deliberately to bring freshness to the lyrics about the alienation of life on the road. Almost no one, apart from old and grizzled Stones' fans, recognise the song. This can be the fate of your talk – *you might as well just have delivered the chorus as most of your other points have never penetrated the audience's brains!*

The one thing we do remember in the Stones' original is the chorus – 'I can't get no … satisfaction'. The lesson is to have strong 'choruses' in your talk. It could be an essential point you want to reiterate, on a slide or verbally, anticipating that if this is all they take home, at least it's the *main* point.

A charismatic maths teacher I know uses this chorus effect in his lessons on quadratic equations. (Yes, maths can be 'rocked up', too!) All the time he is teaching the theory – the verse of his song – he is thinking how to return to the chorus. Which is what? That this knowledge has practical applications in the world of science, technology and construction. His 'chorus' is to bring the class back to the topic of *why* and *how* these concepts are useful, with real examples.

Without some way of relating the storyline of the verse to either the experience of the group or the practical uses of the information, it may all float away like paper cups across the universe. But they'll remember your chorus, if you make it clear and loud. They may even begin to sing along a little, at least in their own heads.

## 'So what?' choruses

One type of chorus is a 'so what?' passage. I've just given the group an idea, notion or model (the verse) and now I need to bring it back to a chorus. At times, I may get their voices into the room, asking them whether what I've said:

- Makes sense?
- Is recognisable?
- Is relevant (theory linked to practice)?

Verse is the theory; the chorus is then a means to summarise and connect this with the audience's experience and reality. Get the verse right and it may be a straightforward 'yeah, yeah, yeah' from the crowd. Just in case, your central theme needs to be embedded in a chorus. Unlike music, your chorus doesn't have to be the same words repeated, but a reinforcement of your core message, said in a different way.

---

**Break the Rules**

Creative musicians often break the rules. Paul McCartney starts the number one single, 'Can't Buy Me Love' with the chorus, and repeats the trick on 'Eleanor Rigby', a contender for the most haunting pop song of all time.

---

## Call and response

Colleague Robert Maguire engages audiences brilliantly. He's often communicating to a group of sales professionals the control strategies purchasing people* use against them to focus the conversation on one variable alone – price. He goes through the first strategy, gets them to experience it through a quiz or task and then comes to his chorus: 'Who is in charge?' It becomes call and response, a well-known form of audience

---

* He knows what he's talking about: he has been the director of purchasing at a number of well-known companies.

involvement stemming from blues and gospel music, and ultimately plainsong. It's still an essential part of R&B and soul music.

Robert says, 'Who's in charge?' The audience say, or mutter, 'Purchasing'. Then there's example number two, and: 'Who's in charge?' – 'Purchasing.'

The chorus gets stronger every time. It's one of the most direct and effective business presentations I've seen, and truly memorable. He then changes the theme into a higher key: 'So how do we recapture control of the commercial conversation?' The rest is different verses to explore solutions, but the chorus is revisited several times with striking examples and stories.

I'm not advocating that you merely have a strong chorus and no content – that would be all sizzle and no sausage – but that you *start* with planning your chorus. All else leads up to that, and it's a concise summary of your message.

The verses, or main passages of your lecture, can also be 'rocked up' so that they're almost as memorable as the chorus. To do this we'll use the 'power chords' of stories and word pictures in Chapter Three. For now, it's chorus, chorus, chorus.

Another name for a chorus is your 'hook'. Something catchy. Rhyming helps, as in defense lawyer Johnnie Cochran's famous pitch in the O. J. Simpson trial, 'If the glove does not fit, you must acquit.' They did!

'Change' is one of those vague words that are over-used by business leaders. I was helping a client write his big speech to launch an exciting transformation, when I came across research that said couples who *slide* into living together, or even into marriage, are less likely to have a successful outcome than those who *decide*.\* The rhyme became a part of his concluding remarks: 'When we consider the future that lies in front of us, it's clear that we can't *slide* – we must *decide*.'

---

\* Susan Pinker, *The Village Effect* (2015).

This was a crisp phrase to summarise and make more concrete what he'd covered in some detail – it was his chorus.

## The Bridge (or Middle Eight)

A 'bridge' in your talk helps to regain and deepen the audience's engagement.

In music the bridge is a short section of a song – often around halfway through – that breaks up the predictability of verse/chorus. While it's related to the main theme, it's also a departure: it may be in a different key and could be vocals or a guitar blitz. The reason it's there is to deepen the emotional impact of the song, and to stop boredom setting in.

Famous bridges include the one in David Bowie's 'Changes'. When he sings 'strange fascinations fascinating me', it's a subtle change of direction from the main verse/chorus. Also, he's expressing something of his essence – a perennially curious mind which continues to keep up with or even stay ahead of the zeitgeist.*

Then there's the gospel passage in Elvis Presley's 'Suspicious Minds'. Or the part in Springsteen's anthem 'Born to Run' when he sings (or growls) 'girls comb their hair and boys try to look hard'. Then he dies with Wendy – it's an everlasting kiss.

Contemporary artists like Beach House are great exponents of the bridge. Their gorgeous album, *Bloom*, sounds like one long bridge, and is capable of taking you by surprise even after a number of listens.

*New Musical Express* writer Matthew Horton captures the importance of the bridge when he says it's 'whatever the hell the artist thinks they can get in before we're begging them to get to the chorus again. It can be a moment of rare beauty,

---

* He's still winning awards – his out-of-nowhere album *The Next Day* in 2013 showed he hasn't lost his ability to stay in touch with the times.

redemption or doubt ... and at its best is the pivot a classic song revolves around.'*

There is no fixed format to this. A bridge is also called 'the middle eight', but it doesn't always have eight bars – or come in the middle! So much for the precision of musical forms: we'll treat it as a passage essential for recapturing and holding the attention of the group.

## The power of a 'side-story'

Your bridge, or middle eight, can take several forms. It could be a side-story that breaks new ground or deepens the ideas you've been developing ...

Matt Dickinson is an author and film-maker specialising in extreme survival. He's climbed Everest while filming a successful expedition, and been on over forty wilderness trips where making the right choices is a matter of life or death. Fortunately, Matt has so far made the right decisions! He's also an in-demand professional speaker on the subject, drawing out lessons for team development and the management of risk that leaders can use in their own enterprises.

His story of the Everest ascent is compelling in itself: the unexpected storms, the death of climbers in rival expeditions, what happens when you pee at sub-zero temperatures; all add colour to the tale.

About halfway through, Matt will introduce a middle eight passage.

❝ Midway in my presentation, I break out from the nitty-gritty details of climbing Everest. I talk about the tragedy of a dead climber called "Green Boots" who we found high on the summit ridge. Up until this point I have focused on my own experience of the mountain, but

* 'Eight Magnificent Middle Eights', *NME* (26 September 2012).

for five minutes or so of my presentation, I talk about this fallen climber that we found, giving the audience a chance to experience *his* story. By outlining the sequence of events that led to this talented climber losing his life, the audience quickly comes to empathise with him and to engage emotionally with a new character. I find this change of viewpoint helps my presentations, giving the audience a break from my narrative and ringing the changes in an effective way.

Then Matt will continue describing his team's ascent, perhaps breaking off after a while into another bridge about the lifestyle, economics and beliefs of the Sherpa people without whom most climbers would have no hope of conquering Everest.

In Matt's Everest talk the bridge echoes and harmonises with the main tune. Just when attention may be wavering in the room, it's a chance to add intensity and vibrancy. An interesting bridge, especially if it contains a strong visual element, can touch the listener profoundly, as well as inspiring curiosity. I nearly wrote that it should create a sense of wonder – that would be overstating it. Piquing the listener's interest is a more achievable goal for most of us. Curiosity will do just fine.

### Your Bridge

You could create your own bridge by bringing one example of what you've been saying to life in more colour and detail. A history lesson about Lord Nelson could benefit from a few enjoyable minutes describing lurid rumours about the life of his lover, Lady Hamilton. This should not be done just with the aim of titillating the sixth form (although *anything* that can titillate the average sixth-former does sound rather tempting), but could be employed as a mood changer, adding understanding about the social and sexual mores of the time.

Beware the horror of the *extended lead solo*. This is where the speaker, thinking this is their chance to shine – as a musical bridge often is – goes off on a ramble about a specific case in far more detail than is necessary. I have seen speakers, especially in the southern European countries, spouting ten-minute monologues or rants that fuzz the mind, giving you total amnesia about the topic.

Maybe I just had bad translators, and I know that cultural norms of communication vary immensely. English is not as musical as the Latin tongues (except for the bits that *are* Latin). It demands shorter, pithier pronouncements. Unless you have a mellifluous voice and a truly gripping tale, shorter is better. The bridge may not be exactly to the point – it may be a tangential story – but it must *support* and *deepen* your point.

## Minor keys and emotions

The bridge may be in a *minor* key. While major keys are thought to be bold, proud and triumphant, minor ones are described as subdued and sad. In Joni Mitchell's 'My Old Man', she sings lovingly about her partner in a jaunty minor key, and then uses a different minor key for the bridge. You sense doubt and unhappiness: it's darker and more reflective.

In the relentlessly upbeat world of professional speaking, it's a risk to move into a minor passage. So you should do it from time to time! I don't agree that the minor segment has to be sad: it's just more pensive, and even gives you the space to express doubts, or more subversively, challenge and question your main argument before returning to the chorus.

Expressing doubts needn't undermine what you are saying. It's more human, and the necessary flipside of rigid certainty. You may describe your own worries about the quality of research on this subject, or your surprise that we are still very much at the start of conquering this challenge: finding a cure for cancer, for example. Alternatively, you could describe moments when you thought you were on the wrong track, and query whether you had been asking the right questions in the first place.

*Inverting* your argument can also open a creative line of thought. When I'm talking about customer loyalty, I might dwell on the *opposite* question: why should customers be loyal if we are not loyal to them?

Don't spend too long on this or it *will* undermine your main theme. But done right, it will add colour, shade and depth to your argument. Whole songs can be performed in a minor key. Take, for example, Steely Dan's first hit, 'Do It Again'. But in a talk, I suggest you reserve it for a few contemplative and reflective sections.

Do you always need a bridge? No, I've been listening to some great songs recently (don't ask), which only have verse, chorus and some interesting guitar, and some that have no chorus. However, it's useful to know about this device, because it's an effective way of creating variety: that's what keeps the listener tuned in.

## Your Climax: Codas and Fades

The way you finish your presentation or class matters.

Now while most presenters and teachers know this, the close all too often takes the form of a summary of key learning or action points. The audience has mentally left the building ...

Here's a common poor end to a talk. The speaker mutters about it being a shame the time is up (listeners may think otherwise) and says,

Well, ... er ... I suppose that's it. Time up. Thank you everybody. Sorry, we don't have time for questions. Or do we? No, sorry, we've run out of time.

In my experience, this happens all too often. A great speaker would never leave the audience on this *note*. (Notice how we naturally use a musical expression, albeit loosely, to describe the mood of the room.) Endings tend to be remembered for their feel, and no one will recall that summary slide of bullet points.

A great climax is what leaves a song – or talk – resonating in our minds in the silence that follows. Radiohead's powerful 'Paranoid Android' is intense enough for most listeners, but in the last minute the scything guitar finale takes it up a notch further.

A coda is the name given to a song's close, from the Italian *couda*, or tail. The tail can have a hell of a wallop to it! To *feel* how this works, in a song or talk, try listening to a number from the strange collaboration between the ironic Sparks and Scottish art rockers Franz Ferdinand, FFS.* The number is 'Johnny Delusional'. It's good, although I have no idea what they are on about, but your attention is drifting until they get to the coda. It's long – a 1, 2, 3, 4 second pause – then the song starts again and builds in intensity. You are hooked and drawn into the finale by the pause.

### Start with the Climax

Most business training, it seems, has the unwritten rule that you must include Maslow's famous hierarchy of needs – from basic survival to self-actualisation. I've noticed that when it gets to self-actualisation, it's always time for lunch! Perhaps because this is the most difficult – though certainly the most interesting – aspect of human motivation to describe. If you have to cover this, I suggest that you *begin* with self-actualisation, and then return to it (with plenty of time before lunch).

* FFS are brave enough to include a song called 'Collaborations Don't Work' on their eponymous 2015 album.

## Rise to a climax

So what can you finish with that's similarly powerful?

Oxford Professor Colin Mayer gives tremendously engaging talks on macroeconomics and the banking industry. In talking about his book, *Firm Commitment*, he explores the takeover of financial institutions by the managerial class, arguing that many of our banks were started by people with a strong sense of social justice – Andrew Carnegie, the Quakers, Lehman Brothers and so on.

His climax? A story about the head of Barclays, Bob Diamond, being grilled by the UK's Treasury Select Committee in the wake of scandals like the rigging of LIBOR. Diamond was already sweating when asked,

> ❛Do you know what principles the bank you head was originally founded on?'
>
> 'Er . . . no, I'm afraid I don't.'
>
> 'Well, let me remind you. They were integrity, honesty and plain-dealing. ❜

You may not have a killer punch like this, though if you practise delayed gratification and take one of your stronger points from elsewhere in your talk, you already have your strong finish. Colin Mayer's vignette also has the benefit of encapsulating the core of what he's arguing.

## Leave them on a high

Your *delivery* may also pick up in intensity towards the end of your talk. But how can you close more memorably? Well, about ten minutes from the end of a one-hour presentation is a marker point for me when I pause and collect myself. I may think inwardly 'strong close'. Whether I do or not, I'm committed to taking it up a notch. If your tone of voice has been more conversational, make it louder. If you've been at the back of the stage, now's the time to move closer. A great music performance pulls the audience in at the climax, psychologically saying, 'Come closer – share this'.

I like to finish on some kind of high. It could be a genuine and emotional thank you to the audience; but if you get the tone wrong or it's scripted, they will know. You can't fool the more musical side of their brains: your tone will trigger harmony or dissonance that circumvents the radar of rational thought. They'll believe you, or they won't.

A relevant story with a funny coda can work here, too, not jokes. Unless the one you want to tell is by far the funniest you and your friends have ever heard (your husband might even have sniggered at it slightly – no, especially *don't* tell that one!). While you can influence the audience's reactions to most things, exhorting them to laugh in the right places is not one of them. And if I sound like Mr Killjoy here, it's because I've witnessed many well-intentioned attempts at icebreaking and closing through humour go awry, including my own.

Exactly when the audience thinks it's all over, that's the moment to take them higher. Think of this as the post-climax climax. There are songs where the music stops; you think it's finished. One, two, three seconds – a long time in the short history of a song – and then it starts up again, building to an even more thunderous crescendo than the first one.

The audience are standing up to leave, and I might say,

Excuse me, everyone, isn't there one thing we've forgotten?

They sit down again and look a little bemused. I might remind them of a question I've planted earlier in the season but failed to answer. (Comedians and storytellers name this a 'callback'.)

I'll ask them to shout out their answers – and then either deliver a passionate rant on the theme, or change the rhythm entirely, sit down on a chair and summarise the essence of the talk quietly and intimately. It might be upbeat and passionate, *or* the contrast of 'going unplugged'.

---

### Health Warning

If you follow this advice too literally, it can come over a bit clunky. 'Here comes the chorus – sing along' would be rather too obvious. Just as the sign of a good cameraman is that you don't notice the camera – you are innocently looking where they discreetly point you – in a talk these elements should be almost invisible. Judicious use of them will affect your audience in subtle ways they are hardly aware of, but they'll feel the positive effects anyway.

---

Cheesy? Yes, if you – or I – follow it woodenly, it could be very formulaic. But putting your attention on the importance of a thought-provoking, warm or provocative close is vital.

If you do have a strong musical ear and prefer, for instance, classical music, you can go deeper and use different paces like adagio and andante passages, the interweaving of motifs and a return to the primary theme, for example. But if, like me, this level of complexity makes your head hurt, use the hooks of successful popular music and you can't go far wrong.

As Bob Marley remarked, 'The thing about music is when it hits you, you feel no pain.' That should be the aspiration for your rocked-up talk.

## Your talk as a whole album

I'm being provocative in advocating the three-minute song structure, although I hope you've seen its effectiveness. Many speakers are using elements of it successfully, consciously or not. Think of it this way: it's seeing your whole lecture from the audience's point of view, putting your attention first on what will keep them hooked.

There are other structures you can apply to your talk to make it feel coherent, like a well-put-together album where the order of the tracks matters. In coaching speakers, I suggest a range of structures. People pick the one that suits their material – and themselves. Structure does matter: it's a map for the listener and a framework for the speaker or teacher to hang their thinking on. However, I have to admit getting bored reading the more worthy guides on this subject. Suspecting you will, too, try this . . .

Make it *simple*. There's a story of an intellectual who was overheard making his points in a restaurant: 'and *ninethly* . . .' I would have checked out round about 'and fourthly'; even sooner, probably. There's a wonderful Gary Larson cartoon with a student at the back of the class putting up his hand to ask: 'Please sir, may I leave now – my brain is full.'

Simple is not simplistic – just as many of the best products are simple (think aspirin and bicycles), so are the best talk structures.

Dylan remarked that he favoured simple song structures because it allowed the emotions to flow through them more easily. Examples of simple talk structures include:

- Past / Present / Future*
- Thesis / Antithesis / Synthesis
- Why? / What? / How will we know we've got there?

* Although, to rock it up a bit, why not *begin* with the future?

Or even simpler:

- Difficulties / Solutions
- Problems / Opportunities
- Misconceptions / The facts

---

### Simplicity Works

'Sound and Vision' is the title of a David Bowie song from his album *Low*. Other musicians have cited this track as an example par excellence of simplicity in song structure. Not simple as in dumb, but very clever in how it manages to build emotion in subtle waves. It's a touchstone for creating a sound picture that can be simply and clearly understood.

---

Then it has to be *coherent*, which is where the album concept* comes into its own. Think of it this way: if you merely present points analogous to your 'greatest hits', with no connecting narrative, you're going to lose them.

## Avoid a 'greatest hits' talk

I saw one of the world's great scientists deliver a 'greatest hits' talk in Oxford. He started by saying, 'I'm going to talk quickly about ten topics that are currently interesting me.' While the audience received the word 'quickly' gratefully, the talk was an underwhelming mess; mobiles were consulted, minds drifted.

A narrative that linked the points, or brief signposts explaining why they were connected, would have helped greatly. That's what I mean by 'coherent'.

* Not the concept album. They can be dire!

The best way to test your talk for coherence is simply to consider, 'Does the audience know why this section links to the next one?' To you it may be self-evident – they may be lost at sea.

Remember the old instruction in science and maths exams: *show workings*. That's what you have to do: share some of your inner thinking on why one point links to the next. You can also make logical links through good use of questions: 'So if X is true, what are the implications?' and 'Up to now, we've only considered the rule itself – what are some exceptions?' Using questions draws the audience mentally into being an active partner rather than a passive recipient of your narrative.

Don't overdo it, or it can feel like the warmer-upper for live TV shows holding a placard saying, 'Laugh now!' Sometimes you want to surprise the listeners with a story, picture or controversial example before returning to put it in context and linking it to the whole. It's your album.

## Psycho-logic

What is the logic that holds together the sequence of songs on an album? Business speaker Brian Weller describes it as 'psycho-logic'. You may not be able to get your mind rationally around why a set of songs – consider those in famous albums like *Sgt Pepper*, *Déjà vu*, *Pet Sounds*, *In Utero*, *Jagged Little Pill* or *My Beautiful Dark Twisted Fantasy* – fit together, but emotionally you 'get' it. Psycho-logic is an intuitive, emotional bond that links your material. When you've put your talk together, try thinking:

- Does it feel like a whole set of ideas?

- Does one idea flow on to the next?

- Are there any harsh jumps in subject matter or levels of difficulty?*

* This is all right if you intend to shake up the audience.

The order of tracks on an actual music album might take into account tempo, key, mood or other variables, as well as ensuring there's an arresting first couple of tracks – analogous to the 'opening bars' of a song – so the listener will want to listen further. One practical way of giving your presentation that 'whole album' feel is to rehearse in *'one take'*.

You may have assembled the pieces of your talk like a jigsaw, but your last run-through should be done *at one sitting*. After all, that's what creates an album that has some unity: it's the psycho-logic of the artist's mood and style at the time of recording. This, more than any tricks, allows you to capture a coherent narrative and mood. It will also help to weed out any parts (points and examples) that feel like filler.*

Surely *Sgt. Pepper*† is a random smorgasbord of styles, you might (rightly) object. Rock, pop, vaudeville, psychedelia, Indian ragas and so on. Your argument would be supported by the fact that the Beatles apparently left the track order to their production team: drummer Ringo Starr remarked that only the first two tracks were conceptually linked. However, even though the sounds came from such varied sources, it does have what one critic describes as a *narrative unity*.‡ It feels of a piece because it expresses the various mind-expanding explorations the band was up to at the time, capturing the zeitgeist for 1967.

Similarly, your presentation will contain what you know and believe *now*, and needs that narrative unity to tie it all together. Does your talk feel just like a set of greatest hits? Well, be a bit pretentious and make it all part of one concept or

* The big criticism of many albums in the age of Spotify and iTunes is that they have two or three good tracks, the rest is just there to fill the album. You will have bits of your talk that are just like that – filler. Or as a colleague critiquing my talks has told me, 'Padding, Nigel, padding.' It has to come out.
† For rock purists, the album was totally inauthentic. For millions, it was nirvana.
‡ Alan F. Moore, 'The act you've known for all these years: a re-encounter with *Sgt. Pepper*'. In Olivier Julien, *Sgt. Pepper and the Beatles: It Was Forty Years Ago Today* (2008).

overarching idea. As long as you carry people with you, they are unlikely to be curious about how you did it. Be bold. John Lennon explains the reason that fans regarded *Pepper* as a concept album: 'It works because we *said* it worked!'*

## Three acts, one story

The well-known **three-act structure** is used by many dramatists and screenplay writers. The notion has its detractors as well as its fans, but used well it can help your talk feel more like a story. It looks like this:

Act 1:   Context / Background / Set-up

Act 2:   The action *rises* until you get to a confrontation, catharsis or revelation

Act 3:   Resolution / Summary

What becomes clear is that you need a riveting way of introducing your theme (Act 1). Act 2 is the longest, so keep it varied and build up to your big point. Act 3 is the last thing they'll remember – what do you want to leave them with?

The movies use this structure extensively. For instance, *Thelma and Louise* reaches its confrontation when the women shoot the rapist, and can't go back to their old lives. Your confrontation – end of Act 2 – may not be so dramatic, but it can still be an anecdote, image or realisation that your talk rises towards. An encapsulation, but not a mind-numbing summary, of what you've been saying, ideally a way of looking at things that will change the audience's perception – and that they will remember.

For me, it might be how I discovered that mindsets can be changed, or a tale of someone overcoming adversity in a way

* David Sheff, *All We Are Saying: The last major interview with John Lennon and Yoko Ono* (2010).

that shames all of us who hold ourselves back by self-limiting assumptions.

From there it's on to the denouement or resolution, Act 3. Hopefully it's not as tragic as Thelma and Louise's last bid for freedom with Mexico in their sights. It's a time to bring together all the strands of your talk, reflect briefly on the journey and signpost what else about the topic remains *un*resolved.

I've seen good science speakers build the tale of a discovery just like the plot of *Thelma and Louise*, the confrontation being the moment of eureka – or failure – of a group of researchers on the trail of a big breakthrough. And, like the movies, you might use the device of starting with a scene halfway through your story – or even your conclusion – before flashing back to the section that says, *Two Years Earlier.*

## Musical examples: from Eminem to Baez

Don't stick rigidly to the three-act structure – there are five-act and seven-step versions if you're really keen – but *do* have a structure. To feel what it's like to tell a story in song, it's worth listening to Eminem's 'Stan'.

The opening (Act 1) colours in the life of the passionate but deluded fan. The cathartic moment occurs outside the main dialogue, revealed when the star receives a message (end of Act 2), then finally and shockingly realises the nature of the tragedy that's occurred (Act 3).

This isn't a spoiler so I won't tell you exactly what happens, except to say there's no neat Hollywood ending. It's better to experience it, even if you know the song. 'Stan' is far more than a cautionary tale about the importance of responding to your post promptly; it has a flow, a forward movement that pulls you up sharp at the end. Eminem uses the three acts brilliantly, as well as taking the part of the two main characters in the story, and duetting with the haunting voice of Dido.

Joan Baez has a wonderful voice, and it's heard to best effect on 'Diamonds and Rust', recorded in 1975. It's a beautiful production, telling the story of her taking a call from Dylan, her former lover, after many years of silence.

In Act 1, he's calling her from life on the road –'a booth in the Midwest'. This first act sets the scene, which is developed as she remembers him, the upsides and downsides of their relationship (that's the diamonds and rust), leading her to a moment of such happiness that she could have died right there and then. That's the end of the action, or of Act 2. When Baez sings 'I loved you dearly', it's hard not to feel goose pimples – her voice is drenched in love and regret.

Finally, she's not having any of it. No chance for him to pick up where he left off: she says that if all he can offer is the same old diamonds and rust, then she's already paid, thank you very much (end of Act 3).

These song examples are to help you get the *feel* of a story told in three acts. If they give you a sense of the need to build in intensity or drama in your own talk, I think the time spent listening will have been well used. Two very different stories, but both artists know how to use the story structure to great effect.

## Rocking up the 'self-help' bit

'Slacker rock' is a musical sub-genre, and most of us are slackers when it comes to the checklists in any book that's meant to be improving our skills.

Let's be honest – confronted with questions like 'Where do you want to be in five years' time?' or 'Can you make a list of your strengths and weaknesses?' most of us press SKIP in our minds. We either quit or go on to the next chapter.

So here's the slacker's guide to the 'things to do and think' that follow.

I've tried to make the activities thought-provoking, to give you interesting and useful ways of applying the ideas in the chapter you've just read.

Next, I suggest you only tackle one or two of the activities. Pick the ones that resonate with you and the material you're working with. They are all connected, so try one or two and the others may also be triggered.

Finally, I've used the different channels we employ to learn anything: reflection, experimentation (trying it out), using our imagination. These are signposted by visuals we're all familiar with, the controls on a music system:

⏮ Rewind (Reflect)

⏸ Pause (Analyse)

▶ Play (Do)

⏭ Fast Forward (Imagine)

## Your Three-Minute Song: Things to think and do

◄◄    Reflect on how catchy your talk is. Put yourself in the audience's shoes: which moments, if any, do you want them to 'sing along' to?

►    Tweet it: summarise your talk in less than 280 characters. Try on the next page ...

►    Map the building blocks of a strong opening, verse, chorus, bridge and climax onto your material.
- Opening bars
- Verse (main themes)
- Chorus (essential point)
- Bridge (attention catching but relevant diversion)
- Climax or fade

◄◄    Think back to previous talks you have given. How much structure and narrative flow did it have, or was it a series of notes or points that just didn't link up coherently? Were there any passages where the audience switched off?

❚❚    Reflect: Does your talk feel like a random selection of points (greatest hits), or does it have a narrative unity (a whole album)?

►    Choose a structure as well as the song-based one. Past, present, future, three acts, or whatever. But *choose*, and summarise it in keywords here.

►►❙    Think of your ending. What are the last words you want the audience to hear, and what state of mind or heart do you want to leave them with?

## Your Three-Minute Song: Your notes

# SET THE STAGE

- ◆ Your Personal Speaking Rider
- ◆ Your Technical Rider (the Strange Case of Van Halen's M&Ms)
- ◆ Visit the Site – Physically or Virtually
- ◆ Sound Check and Rehearsals
- ◆ Researching – and Ignoring – Your Audience
- ◆ Start Me Up: Your First Take

You set the stage well before you speak.

Why are you speaking at all? This might sound an obvious question, but by reflecting on what you believe about speaking and teaching – and creating a personal rider – you will have a more profound understanding of what makes you and your audience tick.

Musicians have technical riders – and you need one, too. Stage fright is best alleviated by careful reconnaissance of the environment, technology and audience. The practical stuff matters: many times I've seen a speaker turn up twenty minutes before their slot, only to find the beamer jumbles their slides and the microphone scratches with every word.

OK, you may not need several pantechnicons of sound and lighting equipment to deliver your talk, but there's still a great deal to learn from how professional musicians prepare the room – and the audience – for their performance. If your mindset is that you can't fix the physical space for maximum receptivity, your self-fulfilling prophecy will come true.

My experience is you have more influence than you think. The likelihood of your talk being successful is enhanced by focused preparation, whether in a formal lecture room or a more intimate classroom. You will become more fluent and natural in your delivery by rehearsing for real.

You also have to 'tune in' to the audience before your speech; we'll cover some useful approaches. This also means having the courage to ignore them on occasion, and dig deeper into your own enthusiasm for the subject.

Finally, it's important to do a 'first take' of your talk early on, allowing your mind to make creative connections from the outset.

◆

## Your Personal Speaking Rider

Speaking is my profession and craft, and *preparing* to speak well is a vital part of the job. I've found that the most fundamental preparation you can do, even before you consider what you want to say, the technology and the environment, is to examine yourself and be able to answer the question '*Why* am I speaking at all?'

Understanding profoundly the *why* will enrich the *how* and *what* of presenting. A few years ago I wrote this down as a personal rider. It's not one I've shared with other people, until now.

It goes like this . . .

I believe:

- Every talk is a unique moment, a one-off.
- Attention is everything: the focus you put into creating a shared experience with this group will be felt and appreciated.
- Enthusiasm is contagious.
- Interaction is possible and desirable, even with several hundred people in the room.
- Audiences want it to be a success.
- This session must be better than the last one I gave!
- Any topic can be 'rocked up' to good effect.
- When I stop improving, I'll quit.

Yes, I felt self-conscious when I first wrote this out. You don't have to show yours to anyone else – create your own personal rider.

Asked to single out the most important item on my list, it would be the one about always improving on the last time. Any interesting musical artist feels this inner desire to learn something new, do something more or simply play better. David Bowie started off as a novelty artist. It's probably best not to recall 'The Laughing Gnome'.

'Stagefright' is a song by The Band, possibly about Dylan, possibly not. I don't particularly suffer from stage fright, but I am moved by the line describing how when the singer has finished, he wants to get right up there and start again!

That's often how I feel. Rarely do we nail it perfectly, so it's always worth noting what you could do even better next time: it's continuous improvement built into your speaking.

## Your core strength

By creating your personal rider, you have set some powerful criteria to self-test the quality of your talk. What are you saying that you've never said before? How lively is your style? What's your own passion for the topic, and how are you going to make it come alive for your audience? These are the kinds of questions you need to be asking of yourself – and answering.

Another way to usefully reflect on your own speaking style is to decide what your core strength is. You get this awareness from feedback: a colleague who knows you well may be the best source of this insight. For me, the penny dropped when a co-presenter told me that I was continually **making connections** between theory and practice, the general and the specific, my ideas and the relevance to the audience. I'd never really thought about it before, and this perception has helped me to play on and strengthen this ability.

Since then, I've got speakers to identify their own core strength. Here's how some individuals have described it:

- Simplifying complexity
- Injecting humour
- Speaking convincingly
- Clarifying stuff
- Just enthusing!

Know what this unique ability is, and it will help to amplify the power of your talks. Two words is not a fixed formula, but be concise.

## Your Technical Rider (the Strange Case of Van Halen's M&Ms)

When a music star is booked they send to the organisers of the event their 'rider' – a list of requirements covering a myriad of technical specifications, preferred snacks and alcoholic beverages and so on. Perfectionist performers are fussy about their requirements, above all because they want to feel free from worry about practical arrangements, so they can devote their attention to performing. (Although you will know hubris has struck if, like Jennifer Lopez, your rider demands a room with all white furnishings, a white grand piano and white roses.)

So why is rock star Eddie Van Halen relevant here? His rider to concert organisers, along with very detailed instructions, contained the request to provide a large bowl of M&Ms – *but with all the brown ones removed!*

Trivial? Yes, but it was more a test than a real need. He discovered time after time that if they hadn't attended to *this* detail they'd probably ignored other more important stuff as well. Sometimes this was a serious problem: in one case the concert organisers hadn't tested the load-bearing strength of the stage when the band's heavy speakers and other equipment were placed on it. The stage collapsed.

The bowl of M&Ms contained brown ones.

This is not entirely rational, though it works. When I am planning a speech, I send the client a video clip a week or two before. It's not in the tidy PowerPoint format – it's an MP4 – and I enclose a clear note that their AV team has to integrate it into the main presentation. It's a Van Halen moment: normally I find that if they've ignored this instruction, they haven't attended to other details such as the placing of plasma screens, the seating layout, etc, and it puts me on my guard. In one case, the room was dirty, the microphones inadequate and the seating plan for the delegates was missing. They hadn't fixed the video . . .

I may not even use the film, but if they haven't fixed it, I will be extra vigilant in attending to the other details. I will arrive earlier in the morning than the conference technical crew.

Now this could easily be taken too seriously and become just a silly game. But just thinking of the image – Van Halen's M&Ms – is a handier reminder of the need to chase perfection than any number of abstractions about quality or excellence. On a daily basis, you and I are faced with numerous moments when we would accept 'good enough'. Applying that extra vigilance will improve whatever you're doing, whether it's writing a report, articulating an idea or planning a presentation. Take a Van Halen few moments each day, and you'll find you're a small step nearer perfection.

## In praise of micromanagement

Micromanagement can be a very good thing! Usually this is seen as the worst crime a manager or leader can commit. It's perceived as undermining the authority of those who are supposed to be doing the job, and can mean the leader has lost the big picture – and the plot.

However, some of the most successful leaders do have a strong streak of micromanagement in them. Steve Jobs had a visionary grasp of the many industries he helped to transform, and was famous for his absolute focus on improving simply everything, not letting anything go to production unless it was as near perfect as possible. It might be the placement and feel of a button, the colour or logo on a piece of technology. It had to be perfect.

Although some individuals suffered as a result of his abrasive interference, the lesson of following through on every detail has become ingrained in the company culture. At Apple conferences, the attention to detail in the arrangements, the graphics, the screen and font size and the whole experience, is second to none. Brown M&Ms are *not* left in the bowl.

The type of things speakers specify in their 'rider' are:

- Mikes. Which type? Hand-held, wireless, lavalier, etc.
- Your computer – or theirs?
- Podium. Yes? No?
- Hand-held remote changer or cuelight for AV team?
- Placement of screen. (Angled to the side can help in a smaller presentation because then the focus is on you, not the screen.)
- Room set-up.
- Cables / wires / computers.

This is just to give you an idea. The last item especially can be interminably detailed with specifications about VGA cables, connectors, adapters and so on. It's one of life's great mysteries – why in a wireless world do we need so many wires?

What's the word you never want to hear a technical person say? 'Should' is a warning. 'This *should* connect.' 'It *should* work.' Here's where I want to be a diva and shout, 'Should ain't good enough.' Then I reflect that perhaps I wasn't clear enough in the first place ...

Common sense may be, as Picasso remarked, the enemy of creativity, but it's very useful here. Have a list,* but hone it down to what's essential. Just as important is to be a polite but determined pain in following through and making sure the person who can fix it has got your instructions.

## Visit the Site – Physically or Virtually

Jake Stevenson is a concert planner for one of the world's biggest rock stars. He visits the venue where his ultimate boss will perform up to three times before the concert. He checks everything from the strength of the stage to the lighting and sound system,

* For examples, contact production company Partytecture (partytecture.com).

the route along which the band will make their entrance, power cables, lines of sight for the audience and so on.

Now this degree of preparation might seem completely unrealistic if it's just you and a memory stick. Especially if you're going to be addressing five people in the marketing team of a major retailer, or a classroom of high school students. There's no band backing you, not much in the way of visual pyrotechnics or audio quality to get right. Surely the AV is already taken care of, the room setting is unchangeable, so there's nothing to fix.

Wrong. Here's how we can learn from the cool professionalism that underpins an inspiring concert.

Visit physically if you can, like Jake Stevenson. Many of my presentations are in foreign venues, so I'm unlikely to be able to pop into the conference centre in Shanghai before I have to deliver a talk to two hundred people. So I visit virtually by looking at plans of the room, liaising with a production team (if there is one) and discussing with the client. When I can't do a Jake and be there physically, I may talk to someone who has used the location.

---

### Glastonbury Preparation: Mick 'n' Keef

When the Rolling Stones were getting ready to headline the world's top modern music festival in 2013, Mick Jagger worked with a personal fitness instructor for weeks. Guitarist Keith Richards said he would also prepare intensely – by making sure all his lighters were full!

Having said this, he and the rest of the band rehearsed their two-hour performance for weeks. The Stones may be one of the most successful live bands of all time, but they still 'set the stage' by rehearsing like hell. Musicians develop muscle memory through their rehearsals, which allows their bodies to take over and play semi-automatically. The same is true when preparing for a talk.

You can also consider what kind of atmosphere you are trying to create – highly involved and interactive, receptive, mainly listening and so on. To achieve this feel or tone, the environment has to support it. To encourage creative dialogue, which you can do even in groups of several hundred, it doesn't help to have delegates seated in formal rows. Try circular cabaret tables, or groups surrounding low coffee tables. A high and distant stage is also not conducive to engaging with the audience.

These are all elements you can influence. They make a subtle but noticeable difference to how the music of your talk is appreciated by the audience. Never walk into the room half an hour before, and hope it will all be hunky dory. It won't be. If you are still in the room fixing slides and microphones just before you speak, not only is it unprofessional, especially if people drift in early, but it also creates unnecessary anxiety that diverts you from getting ready, psychologically, to speak.

I know I'm painting a bleak picture here – hopefully it will be much better than that, especially in a top-end provider. But in my experience, 'hopefully' is not good enough. There's a wonderful quality to the sleep you have the night before speaking in a well-prepared venue, which will reflect in your own confidence and relaxation. Your mind is on what it should be: your message, the way you deliver it and, of course, the audience.

In setting up the room, I'm a professional furniture mover first, a speaker second. I will physically move tables, chairs, a lectern or whatever it takes to fix the environment for maximum receptivity. I'll be an extra pair of hands if necessary to get the job done.

## A Little Paranoia

I have one golden rule with venues: I demand that the room is set up the night before. This is a particularly important instruction if the event is in a hotel, most of which claim to be in the conference industry, but are actually in the business of providing beds and meals. The staff may not know a beamer from an overhead projector and have possibly outsourced the provision of AV equipment to an outside company, who has dumped on them some outmoded kit that no one in the hotel knows how to operate properly. It's better to learn this the night before than five minutes before your talk.

If your wishes are adhered to and the room is ready the night before, you can then rehearse in the actual space!

Surely setting up the room is just basic stuff? Yes, although it's necessary to prepare the ground. This can't on its own make for a great presentation, any more than exciting cover art can make for a great album, but if wrong, it can stop you in your tracks. Think of this physical space planning as a way of tuning in, to being fully present and a relaxed worrywart about getting the details just right.

You might also think of this scene-setting, less elegantly, like a tom cat peeing to mark out his territory. However you accomplish it, you have to make the patch yours. Getting the environment right is one solid gold way of respecting the audience.

You may think this is over-the-top advice if you're in an educational institute, teaching in musty classrooms or lecture theatres. I disagree. A venerable body I belong to organises talks with some of the world's most interesting people, from scientists to politicians to celebrities. Unfortunately, the audio-visual system is almost Dickensian with scratchy mikes, or sometimes no mikes, in a large hall with poor acoustics and antiquated projectors which often don't work.

Now while I recognise that these organisations have far more limited funds than big companies, their raîson d'être is surely to communicate their information, knowledge and wisdom clearly. It's one part of the budget it's foolish to cut.

## Sound Check and Rehearsals

Another lesson from Jake Stevenson's rock band preparations is the sound check. Yes, you do need to check the microphones, and the acoustics if a mike isn't required. You also need to check the visual aspects. Typically I sit at the back of the room and ask one of the audio visual team to stride around the stage – to be me – observing where there are blind spots and where 'I' will move in and out of the light. You are preparing from the audience's perspective, grooving your mind to adopt their viewpoint, literally and figuratively.

One way in which a rock performance differs from a talk is that at a concert there will be security barriers and staff to ensure people can't rush the stage. At a talk you have to think the opposite – how to *remove* the barriers between you and your audience. For me this means getting the podium out of the way and moving the audience nearer. I like to leap off the formal stage, if there is one, especially enjoying the mild panic of those in charge of health and safety. But if you do so and find no lighting on your face, it's not going to work so well.

In a large venue, lighting is critical. What effect do you want to create? If it's conversational, I make sure the house lights are at least halfway up in the room. As well as being seen, I like to *see* people, rather than imagining they are there like a cinema crowd in the dark. We all know what cinema audiences get up to.

> **Camera Tip**
>
> In *RYP* I'm mainly talking about live presentations. But if you're giving a presentation to a camera, as so many of us are on video links and webcasts these days, here's a useful tip. The cold eye of the camera will give you no feedback, the subtle signs that tell you if you are reaching your audience.
>
> Have one or two people stand behind the camera, giving engaging and appreciative facial and physical signs that they are listening intently. Surprisingly, this will bring you to life as well: the warmth of a human connection beats the dead feel of a camera lens every time.

## Put on your audience 'fat suit'

Another practical way of picking up the atmosphere in the room is to sit in on talks before your own. You may have to – it might be a corporate event where you want to make some live links from the Marketing Director's presentation to your own. Observe closely, as you listen to the content, how the dynamics of the set-up work. For instance, does the speaker always stick to one side of the room, leaving out half the audience? Is there a delay on the slide clicker? Does the microphone work equally well for those at the back? Are there any feedback spots? Also sense the 'feel' of the group. Are they already rocking, fully engaged, or are they getting impatient for something more riveting?

In doing this, you are donning your audience 'fat suit'. Health professionals working with obese patients have used this device to develop greater understanding and empathy. Spending a morning wearing a padded outfit – a fat suit – to experience their patients' everyday challenges, like simply getting dressed, making a snack or walking up a flight of stairs, helps them to attune themselves better to their charges.

Similarly, you are checking what it all looks, sounds and feels like from the audience's perspective. While it's not easy to evaluate exactly how this will change your talk – it's definitely as much about sensing as analysing – my experience is that it helps to build sympathy and a little empathy with their point of view.

---

### 'Fat Suit' Your Own Presentation

Watching a video of yourself speaking can be horrible – though normally the horror is outweighed (slightly) by the fascination.

Mentally make your 'fat suit' that of a bored and uninspired delegate: look through their eyes for the ways you deepen their ennui – or shake them out of it.

Have a stiff drink.

Repeat.

---

## Rehearse and re-hear

Rehearsal is a key component in preparing for a musical performance – and it applies to speaking, too. The best run events I've attended were where the company team had spent the day before – or even two days – rehearsing in the actual room, practising and improving on each other's presentations. Think of this like a band rehearsal; if the guitarist is slightly out of tune or the drums too much at the front of the sound mix, now's the time to fix it. Does the Finance Director have incomprehensible graphs? Then the rest of your management 'band' must act like untutored audience members and challenge.

Famed management authority Peter Drucker – the man who presciently called us 'knowledge workers' – was once asked why, late in life and in failing health, he still continued to lecture.

'How do I know what I'm thinking until I hear what I'm saying?' was his insightful response. Teaching is the best way to learn most things, and we all know that strange sensation, in the middle of explaining a concept to others, of really 'getting it' ourselves.

---

### Preparing to Pitch

Much of this preparation might seem less relevant if you are walking into a small conference room, say at a client's offices, to deliver a pitch for a new piece of business. However, even here you can prepare the stage. Get there an hour before, make friends with the secretary, make it home territory.

Care in thinking about where to seat people helps also: if there's more than one on your team, you may want to mingle your people with the client's to create the effect that you are working *with* them rather than *for* (or against!).

Even better, create 'home advantage': use your conference room or a quirky but appropriate venue where you can set up your own conditions for success. Research suggests that ideas put over when you have home advantage have a higher hit rate.

---

Often I rehearse to friends, the cat or the mirror. Then rehearse again. If you're driving, that's also a great time to do it over and over; no one can hear you scream. Best are rehearsals where you only look fleetingly at your notes. Make mistakes – lots of them. This is the time to do it.

Can you over-rehearse, so it comes over all pre-programmed and staid? Yes, I suppose you can, but neither I nor any of the speakers I've quizzed on this point have ever rehearsed enough to experience this problem!

**Rehearse Your Ad Libs**

There's a famous story of Winston Churchill practising his speech for the next day in the Commons out loud, while walking through the corridors of Whitehall. When asked what he was up to, he replied, 'The best ad libs are far too important not to be rehearsed.'

## *Researching – and Ignoring – Your Audience*

Here's the ideal. Meet with or speak to a cross-section of people before the event. Face to face is best, but unlikely in practice. Thirty-minute telephone interviews with half a dozen people – a diagonal 'slice' of the audience – is insightful if you can make the time to speak to them. Use Columbo-type dumb questions like:

- What would you find useful to know about this topic?
- Why do you come to a talk like this?
- Tell me about a day in your life.
- What's the buzz/joke/main topic of conversation among your colleagues or fellow students today?
- What are the 'elephants in the room'?
- What more can I read or research to understand the organisation's or audience's problems better?

At the very least, I make sure I'm thoroughly briefed by the client, asking them to begin with the desired result, and then work backwards. Specifically I ask:

- What do you want people to go away thinking, saying, feeling and acting like that's different or better than when they arrived?

- What's your 'nightmare scenario' for this talk?

The first question is useful because you pick up the tone that's required. They want them to leave thoughtful and reflective, upbeat and inspired or whatever.

Strangely, it's the nightmare question that's the most revealing. The most common responses I get are:

- Dry detail/too much theory
- Message not connected to the audience's reality
- Dull delivery
- Waste of our precious time

Clear enough. What may also emerge is a description of previous speakers who have either nailed it or completely missed the mark. In the latter case, you can enjoy a little schadenfreude, while planning how to escape this fate yourself!

I'm looking for what's preoccupying the delegates and organisers of the event. In business, it could be this year's restructuring, a competitor who is eating their lunch, the retirement of a popular leader or the threat of missing financial targets.

Whatever it is, you need to show some knowledge and even empathy for what they are going through. The credibility of your message will also be enhanced by demonstrating a grasp of key details, numbers and events. Although I don't need to be briefed in as much detail as when I'm wearing my consulting hat, there's a minimal amount of information that is needed to cross the 'so what?' and 'should I be bothered to listen?' barriers in the audience's brains.

## Ignore the audience!

That's the logical stuff – now let's rock up our approach a bit. Sometimes we need to challenge the old advice to 'know your audience' – and try ignoring them instead.

I don't mean this literally, like guitar hero Eric Clapton in his very early days: still learning, he would prefer to play with his back to the audience.

What I am saying is that you shouldn't appease or try too hard to get the audience to like you – and your content. It's *your* material, and beyond a certain amount of tailoring to demonstrate you know who they are, and why they should be interested, you have to plunge into your own thing, even at the cost of losing a few people.

No one will remember, 'Oh, he was very pleasant.' They *will* recall the conviction and enthusiasm you put into your delivery, and the way you connect your ideas to their reality. This is expressed visually in the illustration 'Mind the Gap' (below).

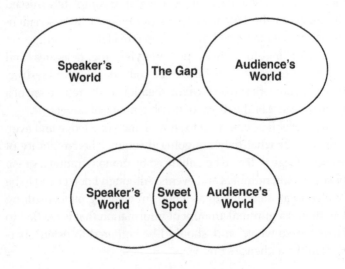

## Mind the gap

You are, of course, trying to bridge between your world and theirs sufficiently for them to learn new knowledge or a fresh way of looking at things – why are they there otherwise? But even at the risk of some unpopularity, you have to give most attention to your own theme to pull them in to that sweet spot.

Charismatic poet and business presenter David Whyte is great at sticking resolutely to his theme. He speaks, surprisingly, on poetry and leadership, and is in huge demand globally. A vital ingredient of his talks is to recite by heart several poems, often repeating key lines to emphasise the musicality of the words and the insights he wants to explore with the group.

---

**Your Wonderwall**

'Audiences quickly switch off when they are talked **at**. Far better to share your own sense of wonder and hope that some of it rubs off. The moment you tell an audience "here is something that I think will interest/inspire/astonish you", you have probably lost them. If, however, you attack a presentation by sharing what **you** are interested, inspired or astonished about, then you have a very good chance to switch them on to your theme.'

Author and speaker Matt Dickinson

---

I was sitting in on one of David's presentations to senior bankers at Oxford University's Saïd Business School, where he and I were Associate Fellows. Not the obvious audience to gain inspiration from Rainer Maria Rilke or Robert Frost, you might think. About ten minutes in, one of these masters of the universe tried to ask a question.

'I'm not taking questions for about twenty minutes,' David replied politely but firmly. 'Firstly, I want to build up a different conversation in the room; one with a different linguistic gravitational pull.' Wow! For the next half-hour it was as if a spell had been cast over the group. The quality of their attention deepened noticeably.

Contrast this with a talk I attended by a famous philosopher speaking in honour of another famous philosopher, now deceased. Right at the start he invited the audience to interrupt and ask questions *at any time*. Sounds open and friendly, doesn't it? But it became a meandering mess, with no coherent narrative.

There are limits to audience participation, and your aim should be to create some resonance, mood or tone in the room, at least in the first ten to fifteen minutes (much less in a pitch). Otherwise people are either switching off or responding from the mindset they brought to the meeting, not the one you want them to go away with.

A band doesn't usually ask for requests two or three numbers into their set. For good reason – it's too soon, and the crowd will only ask for what they already know. Build an atmosphere first, and then the kind of questions you receive will be fresher and more relevant to your theme.

Musicians sometimes believe they are playing for themselves. In case you think it sounds self-indulgent, it's far from playing *with* themselves. When you put your all into what you know, continually trying to find better and clearer ways of communicating it, only you know whether you're doing it better this time. You're competing against yourself.

Another insight from David Whyte's delivery is that he knows the poems he recites by heart. 'By heart' is a very instructive phrase; it's not just remembering the lines, but investing them with an intensity that brings the meaning alive.

We confuse the dullness of learning 'by rote' with the special quality of knowing 'by heart'. There are quotes, lines of poetry and relevant stories that I do suggest you learn *by heart*, and never read from the page. You don't expect a musician to be reading their own lyrics. Knowing some passages and quotes by heart will help you attain that sweet spot.

Learning by heart ≠ Learning by rote!

## Start Me Up: Your First Take

Let's now think about a creative shortcut to set the stage *mentally* – to start on the content of your talk.

Suppose you have an important presentation or talk to give in the next few days or weeks. You probably do, don't you? Some of your ideas are fully formed, others more hazy. You've scheduled some time a day or two before the delivery date to really get to grips with your material, and the overall sensation you have now is one of low-grade background anxiety.

To reduce your stress levels and get you started, we can take inspiration from the world of music. Recording artists are very familiar with the idea that the first take of a song has a certain freshness and intensity to it, while in a later, more rehearsed version the imperfections may have been ironed out and the raw energy of the first take is lost.

A striking musical example of a song that is practically a first take is the single that *Rolling Stone* magazine voted the best of all time: Bob Dylan's 1965 game-changer, 'Like a Rolling Stone'.* For completists, it was actually the fourth take with that set of musicians, but eventually regarded as superior to many of the later ones. The snare shot launches the number, and swiftly the organ and guitar pick up and support the rolling rhythm.

The organist was Al Kooper, a musician who was so desperate to get on a Dylan record that even though he was only meant to be watching, he sat down and played the organ.

---

* Surely some conflict of interest here, but it was a global Number 1!

It's an instrument he claims he wasn't familiar with, and he describes how he was an eighth of a note behind the band, waiting till he heard the chord before hitting the keys!

There were eleven more takes after this one that didn't make the cut – it was the unusual organ sound that Dylan wanted to hear higher in the mix.

Doing the first take with your presentation or talk means imagining you have to deliver it *tomorrow*. Take an hour – two if you can – to throw down all you know about the topic very soon. Even better, list, draw, doodle, type or keyword your ideas *now*. Mind-mapping is great if you know how: use colours, visuals and keywords.

Your focus should be on capturing the *content*, the 'what', rather than dwelling on the 'how', or the way you're going to organise it. Acknowledge the part of your brain that wants to dwell on fine detail, or put it in sequence, and tell it you'll come back to this later. Wait till you've more or less emptied your mind on the subject before you do.

Only then assemble your material in the rough order you plan to give it. Number and head the subsections. Decide which areas need more research or thought. Now imagine you're in the studio, the clock is ticking, and you have to at least lay down your backing track – a rough first take.

### Having Trouble Starting? Use Bowie's Random Method

Sometimes it's useful to get your mind off its familiar tracks and preoccupations to allow fresh thinking in. David Bowie did this with his cut up method (probably derived from novelist William Burroughs's even more random approach).

Bowie would cut out headlines or phrases that appealed to him, saved from a wide variety of publications. Then he'd stick these on a board, move them around, and see if any of the ▶

items or their connections sparked his creativity. Some of the phrases became lines in his songs.

You can also use this in creating a talk. I've tried it out on a few occasions, usually with fruitful results. Writing one talk entitled 'Can We Really Invent the Future?' I came across these two lines in a magazine:

'The physical impossibility of death in the mind of someone living' (a Damien Hirst art piece).

It started a great conversation about the difficulty of imagining the future.

'Working backwards from the future' (a sub-heading in a technology article).

Again, this triggered thoughts about the need to visualise the future first, and only then work towards it.

Two things become clear at this stage. The first is that you almost certainly know more than you thought you did, and mapping your ideas in this first rough form will alleviate some of that free-floating anxiety.

The second advantage is that you are clearer on *what you don't know* and need to work on further.

Now your creativity can start to flow. Your mind will begin working on solutions even while you're engaged in other activities. The brain is primed to notice what it's incubating through the magic of selective perception. Remember what it's like when you come across a new word, film or book title? Suddenly it's everywhere – you turn on the TV and it's mentioned. Open up the paper and there it is again.

Without any conscious effort, your mind is searching for patterns and matches, data that you might have screened out before. Provided we've put the subject matter consciously into the forefront of the mind, we'll be attuned to finding solutions, and fresh and relevant material for our talk.

News websites, newspaper articles, YouTube videos and chance conversations with colleagues will help you fill in the gaps. These will add examples, depth and colour to your talk. Carry a journal or use the notepad on your tablet: connections will now start arriving in your mind, but often at unpredictable moments. Don't think, 'OK, I'll remember that later!' No, you won't. Ideas are like dreams – something we forget every day. Give your thoughts more substance by writing them down, drawing or typing them. 'Out of sight, out of mind' is the old wisdom we're using here; the more visually you can lay out your thoughts, the more effective your mind will be in hunting for creative matches.

You haven't fully written or rocked up your presentation yet, but the first take or rough recording has performed a 'start me up' for your own creative process. When I use this idea in coaching speakers, we are frequently amazed how far planning the talk develops just in this first session. Novel ideas begin to pop up even at this early stage. You could be 50 per cent of the way there already!

Of course, this all assumes you have interesting material to rehearse *with*. We'll find different ways of bringing this content to life in the next chapter by exploring the Power Chords of Speaking . . .

## *Set the Stage: Things to think and do*

⏮ Reflect on 'Why I speak'.

▶ Incorporate this into writing your personal rider: what you believe about speaking or teaching.

⏭ Consider what you and your audience need – well ahead of time – to create the perfect learning environment.

▶ Create your own technical rider from this.

▶ Find out as much as you can about your audience's level of interest and understanding about your topic. How are you going to do this?

⏸ Learn by heart. What are the memorable quotes, facts or stories that you need to know by heart, as if you were a performance poet?

⏸ Ignore your audience – think what most stirs you about this topic.

▶ Try your 'first take' today – devote time to drawing, throwing down, mind-mapping or typing your talk *as if you had to give it tomorrow!*

## *Set the Stage: Your notes*

# THREE

# THE POWER CHORDS OF SPEAKING

◆ Story Time!

◆ Paint Word Pictures

◆ Write Great Lyrics

◆ Have Strong Titles

◆ Use Golden Facts

Power chords are simple shapes on the guitar – especially the root notes of a chord – moved up and down the fretboard for powerful effect. Think 'You Really Got Me' by the Kinks or 'My Generation' by the Who and you'll understand the impact, although the technique was used as early as Willy Johnson backing Howlin' Wolf right through to Nirvana and up to the present day. It's also been applied to the equivalent on synthesisers and keyboards.

The connection here is that the shape is essentially the same, but a completely different sound is produced as the hand slides up and down. Similarly, your content – the 'shape' of your talk – doesn't have to change, but by using certain techniques you can invest it with more power and resonance.

We're using the analogy loosely, but the effect is similar in speaking and music: your 'power chords' are methods for making your theme more vital and memorable, in ways that move the listener and stir their imagination.

Let's take the talk you've created so far, and do exactly that with your content . . .

◆

## Story Time!

Stories will hook your audience more than abstractions.

To make this crystal clear, think of the biblical precept to 'love thy neighbour'. (A similar tenet exists in all the world's religions.) Now you could either convey this message in a bullet point – 'be kind to strangers' – or tell the story of the Good Samaritan who actually crosses the road to help someone in distress, while everyone else walks on by.

Which is the more powerful? It's a no-brainer: the story wins every time. It's visceral, memorable and emotional, and you see it played out in your mind's eye, while the verbal concept remains flat and dead on the page. While the scientific theories of a thousand years ago often sound bizarre and even plain wrong – physiology and physics come immediately to mind – the stories used to convey human or spiritual truths are still valid.

The difference between bullet points – for example, 'care for the customer' – and the telling of a story about going the extra mile for the customer is huge. One numbs the mind, the other feeds the imagination. I bet Socrates didn't use bullet points.

Business has long recognised that building a brand is essentially selling a story. As Anita Roddick, founder of The Body Shop, remarked: 'We can't be bothered with strategy – we just tell stories.'

Today, storytelling is undergoing a huge renaissance, possibly in reaction to the arid language of modern science and technology and the slippery and vague nature of words used in politics and commerce.

I would even say there's been an *over*-reaction, with speakers sharing personal or family tales to such an extent that I find my 'so what' meter flashing wildly. I do want to know the *point* of the story, and I don't want to be emotionally manipulated, as happens in much of Hollywood storytelling.

When considering which stories to use, it's worth remembering Steve Martin's words to John Candy in the film *Planes, Trains, and Automobiles*:

> ❝ When you're telling these little stories, here's a good idea: have a point. It makes it so much more interesting for the listener. ❞

## Stories and suspense

The BBC's Reith Lecture, named after its first Director-General, is a treasure trove of great talks by some of the world's leading minds.

Dr Atul Gawande, a surgeon and writer, gave 2014's lectures on the Future of Medicine. His second talk, 'The Century of the System', sounds like dry stuff: tackling the problem of complexity in healthcare.

Within two minutes he has hooked you by the tale of a three-year-old Austrian girl who drowns in a pond. It's thirty minutes before she's fished out of the lake and she doesn't draw a breath for an hour and a half. Surely she is dead? Amazingly, thanks to the skill and brilliant co-ordination of over a hundred people, the little girl is slowly revived and eventually makes a full recovery.

Dr Gawande describes the difficulty of emulating this success in other medical emergencies, given the sheer complexity and expense of modern models of care. The successful outcome was achieved more through systems than medical expertise. For the right physician to be prepared to receive the patient at exactly the right moment, where minutes could be the difference between life and death, a healthy recovery or permanent brain damage, was all about having the right system in place.

His forty-minute talk concludes with a shorter, but similar story bearing out the truth that for the system to work in these cases, the critical person in the chain is not the doctor, but the telephone operator! And the tool they need to co-ordinate resources efficiently enough to save a life? A checklist! Yes, a very well-thought-through checklist, but a list just the same. It's a powerful and surprising climax.

The 'sandwich story' illustrated here means encapsulating your concepts in a tale at the start and finish. Naturally it helps if listeners can immediately connect with it – we can all feel the anguish of the parents as their three-year-old child is fished out of the lake, apparently lifeless.

The initial story contains the DNA of the whole argument, and is used as a thread or motif throughout the talk; finally it's returned to at the end to remind the listener that this is a tale with deeply personal, human implications.

Suspense is a key part of storytelling. You can leave the tale unfinished in your introduction so that people want to listen further to discover the ending. The story creates a red thread throughout the talk, and allows you to return to and reinforce your central point with more intensity at the finale.

## Teaching stories

Teaching stories work, too. Unassuming and soft-spoken Richard Pascale, a highly regarded business educator and thinker, has a great tale to tell. *The Power of Positive Deviance**  is the book he co-authored with social change pioneers Jerry

---

* Richard Pascale, *The Power of Positive Deviance* (2010).

and Monique Sternin. Their revolutionary approach to serious problems as varied as child malnutrition, infant mortality and female circumcision is to focus on the exceptions – the 'positive deviants' from the norm – and use this insight to communicate solutions to the wider population.

Investigating child malnutrition in Vietnam, they discovered that there were a few children who were not malnourished, despite living in exactly the same economic conditions as the majority who were. On careful inspection, there was a tiny but significant difference in the diets of these positive deviants. Their mothers were feeding them food available to all, but disregarded by most: tiny shrimps and crabs, no bigger than a fingernail, from the paddy fields, mixing them in with the rice. Sweet potato greens, commonly regarded as low-grade fare, were also thrown into their meals.

When this insight was shared, not without difficulty, with the wider population, there was a 65 to 80 per cent reduction in malnutrition among those reached.

Now it took me a fair few words to give you just a flavour of the positive deviance philosophy. But, to Richard its essence is simply: Invisible in plain sight.

No one had seen the solution because they were looking in the wrong place, trying to tend to those who were malnourished, rather than looking to those who weren't. 'Invisible in plain sight' is an example of a phrase that's almost a story in itself.

Nothing beats an actual story: the DNA of the positive deviance approach is brought to life by the authors in a tale of the well-known Sufi sage, the Mulla Nasrudin. The Mulla was continually leading a chain of donkeys across the border. The border guards searched the saddle bags carefully every time, expecting to find contraband – it was known that Nasrudin was quickly becoming a rich man, so he must be profiting from these frequent trips. They searched thoroughly, never finding anything.

Years later, Nasrudin was taking tea with the retired border official who'd been so keen to bust him. The old man was still curious, and couldn't help asking:

> ❝ Nasrudin – we're both long retired now, so we can talk freely. I knew you were smuggling something valuable past me. You can safely tell me. What was it?"
> "Donkeys," replied the Mulla. ❞

Tricking the listener out of their usual thinking patterns is another aim of this kind of story. Zen tales are aimed at out-flanking and subverting rational thought, and they are a good source to explore if you want to rock up your talks, and make people think.

The most powerful tales are personal ones, because they are likely to touch people more emotionally than the ones I've described so far. You might think about an incident that stimulated your interest in this topic or field. An inspiring teacher, a book, a TV programme or lecture, or quitting school altogether and finding your own way.

All of us have stories like this inside us – they may even be ones we've never really reflected on, or told to another. A personal narrative or story has great power to bring even the driest of subjects alive. The listener is sucked in emotionally, your content becoming three-dimensional as they step into the story in their own heads. We're hard-wired for stories.

*New York Times* science writer Malcolm Gladwell is simply brilliant at turning the abstractions of sociological and psycho-logical research into a fascinating story. Sometimes his aim is to highlight injustice, as in the case of blind prejudice towards the hiring of female orchestra members – reversed when the auditions were held behind a screen.* His storyline brings to life the unfairness of this deeply ingrained gender stereo-

* Malcolm Gladwell, *Blink* (2005).

typing. While the big idea here isn't surprising, the research becomes a living thing when given the story treatment.

You could do worse than to dip into Gladwell again – or other tremendous science writers like Steven Johnson* – to see how they take dusty facts and weave a compelling story around them.

## Find the back story

What if you haven't got much of a story to tell? Then try finding the back story. The back story to an idea, a theory, a person, a product. Or a song, like that behind Joni Mitchell's 'Little Green'.

I'd always liked this song, but without knowing why. Sometimes that's enough, but here, understanding the back story has made me feel its real impact.

'Little Green' is a love song and blessing to the daughter Joni Mitchell gave up for adoption when she was twenty-one. She describes all the birthdays, the joys and sorrows of a life she won't be there for, and her hope that the new family will cherish her little girl. It's like a message in a bottle – a special letter she doesn't know will reach its destination, and all the more profound and moving for that.

The words are infused with such tenderness and sadness that I can't listen without a tear or two. Perhaps it's more relevant to me because I have an adopted daughter, although you'd need to be hard-hearted not to feel *something* once you know the story.

In the same way, you can explore and include the back story of characters you introduce into your talk. What in their upbringing was significant or extraordinary, what experiences fashioned them, what were their dreams and fears? Your main story will appear in sharper relief when you shade

---

* For example, try Steven Johnson's *Where Good Ideas Come From* (2011).

in the background. This will involve research that delves deeper than Wikipedia.

Business has its back stories, too, like that of American entrepreneur Fred Smith, who founded FedEx. His fledgling business was nearly broke, and he'd just failed to secure the money to pay the next round of wages. Instead of flying home from the unsuccessful finance meeting, and just giving up, he took a decision to head to Las Vegas for the weekend and gamble his last dollars. Fortunately for him, his staff and millions of customers subsequently, he won enough money to pay the wage bill, turning $5,000 into $32,000. This was a lot in 1971, enough to stave off creditors for a few precious weeks, giving him time to get the company on a solid footing.

This back story to the genesis of FedEx adds colour and an edge to what would otherwise have been an unexceptional tale of business growth. It also makes you appreciate the man's chutzpah as well as his skill at blackjack. Who of us would have taken this risky route?

Theories have back stories too. The search for longitude, or the discovery of natural selection are riveting tales in themselves. The concepts have the star roles, and are brought to vivid life by the back stories of seekers involved in creating, or holding back, breakthrough thinking. Even a mathematical formula can be the hero of a story: *Fermat's Last Theorem* by Simon Singh is a striking example.

It's also vital to think about how to 'paint pictures' in the listener's mind through the imagery and words you use …

## Paint Word Pictures

Which do you recall: names or faces? It's a simple, but revealing question. Visual memory trumps verbal every time.*

* There are simple techniques for remembering names. See my book *Rethink: How to Think Differently* (2006).

Your talk is essentially words, even if supported by images and props. The most effective speakers paint pictures with these words. As Anton Chekhov remarked: 'Don't tell me the moon is shining; show me the glint of light on broken glass.'

Using too many abstractions is a sure way of losing your audience. You also need concrete images that they can see, feel or touch, more like forgettable names than memorable faces.

Poet and musician Leonard Cohen is gifted in creating visual images with his lyrics. His son, Adam, tells of his father's intense focus on creating an 'objective correlative'. In other words, instead of saying 'it's late', what about: 'They're hosing down the sushi bar.'* You can *see* it's late. It's like the glinting of the moon on a surface, rather than saying, 'The moon is out.'

Even politicians sometimes get this right. Instead of talking about the unreliability of self-censorship and self-monitoring of press standards (I imagine you had trouble paying attention to that!), you could say, 'They're marking their own exam papers.' Maybe you could say both – adding the latter word picture gives your listeners an image or scene to remember.


## Build a garage!

So how can you paint more effective pictures with your words? Look through your main ideas. How many of them are mere abstractions, slogans or concepts? In business, words like 'accountability', 'alignment', 'commitment', 'vision', 'purpose' and even 'innovation' fall from the speaker's mouth with a tuneless thud. The music equivalent is listening to the lyrics of say, the Spice Girls. 'I'll tell you what I want, what I really, really want' isn't far from saying, 'We want to create a robust strategic framework for implementing change – going for-ward!' That's what we really, really want!

* Interview in *Uncut Magazine* (3 April 2015).

Replace as many of these abstractions as possible with a sushi bar/'moonlight glinting' physical or sensory image.

I'm often asked to talk about creating an innovative culture in an organisation, potentially a vague topic. My sushi bar word picture is 'build a garage!' Why? Apple, Siebel, Google, Hewlett Packard and Oracle were all born in garages. The economic necessity of working creatively in a cramped intimate space is the magic. Look at the Dilbert cubicle hell of the average office block: can you imagine anyone coming up with a boundary-breaking, high-risk new idea in this stifling environment?

What I'm really advocating is a 'garage mentality', where rapid prototyping, experimentation and an obsession with upending the status quo is the norm. One customer liked the idea so much that they are planning to build a bricks and mortar garage on their site, as a lab for innovating new products!

'Gentlemen, we have no money, so we will have to *think*!' is a wonderful quote from the great scientist, Lord Rutherford, inspiring his research team to solve big problems with scant resources. This is the notion I'm trying to put over in my talk: the idea doesn't lodge itself in the mind so powerfully as the word picture of a real life, concrete garage.

So where are the 'garages' in your talk? Don't overdo it, but see how many abstractions you can give solid form to with an icon, example, story or picture.

Abstract words and phrases slip off the tongue – and out of the mind of the listener – like so many puffs of smoke. They make you comfortably numb. In this vein, a retiring CEO recently summarised her advice to her former company as: 'Execution is primary going forward.'

'Vapourware' is my label for this kind of language. What does it mean? 'Execution' is just doing stuff; 'primary' is very,

very important; but 'going forward'? What other way known to physics can you take an organisation?*

Contrast this with Apple's early and largely successful mission to create products that were 'a bicycle for the mind'. You can *see* that, as well as intuitively relating to an object and experience – riding a bike – that's familiar and trusted.

---

### More Plastic Spoons

Few bands could create mental pictures with such immediacy as The Who during the 1960s. Their subject matter ranged from teenage porn ('Pictures of Lily') to seaside simpletons ('Happy Jack') to the ageist protest of 'My Generation'. One of their most evocative images is in 'Substitute', a story of being second best, an outsider. 'I was born with a plastic spoon in my mouth' tells you something it's hard to forget.

---

## Appeal to the senses

Word pictures are also aided by appealing to any of the other four senses. What are you *hearing* about your topic from practitioners or customers? Can you use some sound bites or videos of their opinions?

Touch can be introduced by having something physical to handle. A sample meteorite, a product or body part.

Smell? Well, you may have to be more figurative, talking about the odour of failure, the smell of success or what it takes to be a bloodhound and 'sniff out' discoveries in the laboratory, or opportunities in the market.

Taste may be the hardest to use directly, but there are useful images that will stick: the notion of an idea appealing to your taste buds, that of an 'aftertaste', the sweet and sour sides of an argument.

* I counted 28 'going forwards' on one two-day corporate leadership event.

There's a cliché about music writing that I can't resist challenging here. It's said that you can't really do it, that it's like 'dancing about architecture'. It's a phrase repeated mindlessly, as if it's self-evident. I guess what it's trying to say is that it's a completely different medium, and that language can't really convey the emotion and feel of a song. Agreed so far, but some writers have the gift of capturing its essence – by painting 'word pictures'.

Nick Drake died in 1974 at the age of 26 leaving behind only three completed albums. And, incomprehensible in the days of YouTube, *no* video footage of him performing. Despite this, there are few singer-songwriters who have had such a profound influence on the following generations of performers. When many stars today are asked that old question, 'Who influenced you?', Drake is high up the list.

Writer Ian MacDonald describes the feel of Nick Drake's sound this way:

> ❝ To listen to Nick Drake is to step out of this world of pose and noise, and enter a quiet oak-panelled room dappled with sunlight – a room opening, through French windows, into a lush garden, quiet because we're in the country, far from the sound of the city. It's summer, bees and birds are abroad in the shade and, beyond the nearby trees, a soft tangle of voices and convivial laughter can be felt, along with the dipping of languid oars in the rushy river winding through cool woods and teeming meadows hereabouts: an English landscape with Gallic ghosts from *Le Grand Meaulnes* and *La maison de Claudine*. And an acoustic guitar playing gently beyond the hedgerow in jazzy 5/4: 'River Man'.* ❞

---

* Ian MacDonald, *The People's Music* (2003).

He's brilliantly captured how the music makes you feel, through the power of imagery. There's no good reason why you can't dance about architecture.

Gravel-voiced Tom Waits hits you in the guts rather than in the mind. Around the time of his 2002 album, *Blood Money*, I read a review that described him as a troll who had found his musical instruments buried in deep marshland, and was using them to try to communicate with the human race.* Wow! This phrase has stuck in my mind while thousands of others have skipped my memory – that's what a word picture does.

Do the same with your talk. If you're describing a scientific discovery, let us have it through all the senses. What did Alexander Fleming's laboratory *look* like? How did it smell? What did he *say* when he first realised the mould growing in his culture plates was a discovery that would create penicillin – and go on to save millions of lives? What did he look like?

Use the senses. Paint the picture.

Stories and images are vital to give form to intangible thoughts. The words or lyrics you use need to be similarly vibrant.

## Write Great Lyrics

The main thread of your speech will be in words; in lyrics, not music. It's an *audi*-ence. So while I've emphasised the rhythmic, musical and visual nature of your talk, there are also techniques, obvious and subtle, which can bring your language alive.

A great sourcebook is Mark Forsyth's *The Elements of Eloquence: How to Turn the Perfect English Phrase*. It doesn't sound

---

* I've tried hard to find the source of this comment. Thanks to whoever wrote this brilliant phrase.

very rock and roll, but it's brilliantly and humorously written, and very useful for the speaker.

Forsyth's theme is that Shakespeare was applying specific verbal techniques to make his language more catchy, well before the Beatles used similar methods to write some of the world's most famous songs. Shakespeare had to work at his craft, often repeating and improving on his earlier efforts as he became a more skilled writer and poet.

Let's start with an easy one: **alliteration**.

I'm not sure why we love phrases where the words start with the same letter, but there's no denying the impact. When Shakespeare writes 'Full fathom five thy father lies' it is of course great poetry, strongly evocative. Mark Forsyth adds:

> ❝ Express precisely the same thought any other way – e.g. 'Your father's corpse is 9.144 metres below sea level' – and you're just a coastguard with some bad news!* ❞

British Prime Minister Tony Blair became briefly popular at the time of Princess Diana's death simply by uttering his press secretary's phrase, 'the People's Princess', in a heartfelt way. Would it have worked as the 'people's idol' or 'role model'? I think not.

Does your company need to Inspire and Innovate, Amaze and Astound or Care and Create? Or do you have the ambitions of a conqueror like Julius Caesar talking about his holidays in Britain: 'Veni, vidi, vici.' Strangely, I don't remember a single other thing he said, except in Shakespeare.

Find a few phrases where you can use easy alliteration. Don't force it, and don't overdo it, or it will come over sounding like the ultimate alliterated chorus:

Yeah. Yeah. Yeah.

---

* Mark Forsyth, *The Elements of Eloquence* (2014).

Then you could also liven up the impact of your lyrics with a figure of speech called the **tricolon.**

The power of three is an old notion, but still has resonance. *Egalité, liberté, fraternité* wouldn't have the same ring if it was just the twins *egalité* and *liberté*. Nor would 'Location, location, location', a phrase that passes for wisdom in the minds of estate agents. Two locations doesn't work: it's the asymmetry of the third one that does. And the third works especially well if it provides a kick in the tail, and creates some surprise:

Lies, damned lies and statistics.

Orators know this stuff: that's why Barack Obama's brief victory speech still managed to pack in twenty-one tricolons. This technique can even be used in a song title, like Nick Lowe's 'What's So Funny 'Bout Peace and Love and Understanding?' or Belle and Sebastian's 'Little Lou, Ugly Jack, Prophet John'. You are intrigued.

My suggestion is no more than three good tricolons in a talk. They may also be part of your chorus:

Q. 'What does this organisation need to innovate?'
A. 'Curiosity, creativity and commercial awareness.' (An alliterative tricolon!)

There are no obvious rules here: just the 'scales' of speaking which can be practised, and recombined in countless ways.

## Read well, speak well

Reading well and broadly is the time-honoured route to bettering your own turn of phrase. Publications like *The Spectator, The Economist,* the *Guardian Weekly* or the *FT Weekend* are worth reading simply for the quality of language used. Focus on language, especially words you don't know – I have my online dictionary to hand – and interesting neologisms. There's something more fluid about learning from constant and curious reading than resorting to a thesaurus, but that can be useful, too. I love the graffiti that reads: Roget's Thesaurus Rules, Governs, Dominates – OK!?

Clichés are the fluffed notes of a talk. However, one person's cliché is another's wisdom, so why not consult a dictionary of clichés. Yes, they do exist – and be prepared to be horrified when some of your own common phrases pop up.

### Beyond the Obvious

Thinking beyond the obvious and the clichéd is essential and as usual the Beatles got there first:

'Listening now to the early records, one is constantly amazed by the ingenuity and skill with which Lennon and McCartney skipped beyond the obvious, using existing styles and making them sound fresh, and creating striking songs with great economy and verve.'

Hugh Barker and Yuval Taylor, *Faking It* (2007)

The word 'issue' is commonly misused, and worse, has become a utility word to insert when you've lost your way – or forgotten your thesaurus. My personal rule is to switch off the radio when I've heard 'issues' five times; it doesn't take long. The meanings it's used to encompass are:

- Difficulty
- Challenge
- Concern
- Argument

- Topic
- Problem
- Disagreement ...

I could go on, but won't. I was shocked to hear a ten-year-old friend of my daughter's describe a badly behaved boy in her class as having 'anger management issues'. My mind was also fuzzed when I visited a client and noticed the tense atmosphere between people in the room: it was 'explained' to me afterwards that there were 'some issues around trust'. That's clear, then!

Perhaps you don't have an issue with issues? Try to give your words the 'fat suit' treatment I described earlier, listening for the mindless, second-hand phrases that we all use.

---

### Clichéd? Moi!?

How do you know your talk has become clichéd? When the sound in your own head lacks conviction. When it seems too obvious even to you – then you've hit the dull note of cliché. If you are saying 'going forward', 'at the end of the day' or 'it's a big ask', or using too many vague words like 'issues', 'challenges' or 'a robust framework', the audience might as well be listening to a half-hour sound check.

Some quotes have been so over-used that they've almost slipped into cliché. I'm thinking especially of Gandhi's remark that 'you have to be the change you want to see in the world'. I've heard this at around half the events I've attended. Look further – find something original and fresh.

## Great quotes

The great lyrics don't have to be all your own. Insightful quotes*
can give authority and depth to your talk. Be more original and
avoid the examples that are so overdone. Einstein's definition of
madness – 'Doing the same thing over and over and expecting
a different result' – has been used so often that I tune it out.
It's a bit like hearing an overplayed song that was OK the first
time, but has had so much radio time that you're bored with it.
Fleetwood Mac's 'Albatross', Pharrell Williams singing 'Happy'
or Adele's 'Rollin' in the Deep' come to mind, regrettably.

There's also something ironic about repeating the Einstein
quote over and over – and expecting people to think differently as a result!

Research a little further than the obvious sources or you'll
come up with elevator music. Especially choose quotes that
you can break down and explore in more detail. I started a
talk on setting priorities to the executive team of an engineering company with comedienne Lily Tomlin's crack that she'd
always had the ambition to be someone, but had later realised
that she should have been more specific in her wishes.

Not only did this raise a laugh, it also allowed me to drill
down into the need for specific, measurable and attainable
goals, as well as reinforcing the point that the future is built
by what we do *now*.

The nature/nurture debate may not have kept you awake
at night, but it's engaged philosophers, scientists and thinkers
throughout the last centuries. An expression that's great for
starting a discussion on this topic is: 'If nature loads the gun,
nurture pulls the trigger!'

There's a ton of research you can link into this apparently
simple statement.

* A good source is the 'Wit and Wisdom' column in *The Week*. They have trawled
through the best articles in a wide range of publications, and you'll find a great
collection of new and old wisdom.

When I'm speaking about innovation, I like the idea from Silicon Valley serial entrepreneur Marc Andreesen that he enjoys people looking at him as if he's said something weird – he takes this as a compliment!

Innovation is always 'weird' in terms of conventional thinking. Andreesen's thought is a launching pad for describing how every innovation – from telephones to laptops to tablets to the cloud – has been vehemently 'yes-butted', especially by the incumbents in an industry, usually just before a wave of disruptive innovation envelops them.

I like the story of the BlackBerry executive who was asked what were the chances of the nascent iPhone threatening his company. 'Vanishingly small' was his pronouncement. Now that's a thought I can explore with a group! A good build on this is investor king Warren Buffett's warning to avoid the ABC of bad business: Arrogance, Bureaucracy and Complacency. Another tricolon.

Don't just repeat quotes. Break them down and link them to your theme.

Love of language is the basis of speaking well, and there are few better tools for you than a good dictionary of word origins. This is not just about being pedantic and knowing the roots of words, it's also about seeing the familiar in a fresh light. Whenever I'm stuck on a topic, I dip into the *Bloomsbury Dictionary of Word Origins*.

Often I'm speaking to technology companies. (Whether an organisation is formally in this industry, 'technology' is the word that's on everyone's lips.) So I searched a number of sources for what the word actually meant.

Any ideas? Probably not. Nor had most people in some of the world's leading companies specialising in this stuff. So much for curiosity.

*Techne* (from the Greek) means, 'art, craft or ingenuity'. At least that's the closest we can come. Now that gives an entirely new spin to the conversation, doesn't it? Especially as the second part, *logos*, means 'the word', or knowledge. Art of the word? I now realise *RYP* is a 'technology' book ...

## Have Strong Titles

The traditional musical advice for a catchy chorus is to include the song *title*. But when your theme is Further Maths, Key Stage Nine, it's going to be hard to get your tongue around.

A great science teacher I know gives her lessons quirky names – 'Why do we need molecules?' or 'Noah's Ark and Evolution'. When she gets it right, it intrigues the class and gives her a 'hook' to hang some of her thinking on: in the first case an investigation of why molecular research is vital in pharmacology, in the Noah talk competing theories of human evolution. Like a chorus, she will return to exploring the title throughout the lesson.

---

### The Perfumed Garden

A life insurance company once advertised a talk of mine as 'The Perfumed Garden'. The hook? The session was about passion for the customer and obsession with the product: Passion and Obsession are well-known scents.

---

One way to come up with a catchy title is to *reverse* the received wisdom on a topic. The book *What They Don't Teach You At Harvard Business School* by Mark McCormack is a good example. Harvard has responded cleverly with a book entitled, *What They Teach You At Harvard Business School*.

The title can be provocative, like *How to Kill Innovation – Our Company Guide* or *Why Richard III Doesn't Matter*. This shouldn't be just showing off: it has to give colour and a sharpness to what you are going to say. And it should usually be short: *She Loves You* may be trite, but it's unforgettable.

A slightly alarming title means you're probably on the right track; much as writing your own CV should make you cringe a little. It means you've put your best foot forward. *Leadership and Strategy*, *The Gerund* or *The Rise of Nazism* are just muzak, and don't start you off on the right note. Rock it up a bit!

Your titles don't need to sugar-coat your topic. I like the way a maths teacher trailered his lesson by calling it 'The Really Difficult Bits in Algebra'! And the safety at work professional who entitled his lecture, 'A Boring Talk About Health and Safety'. Naturally, his message was that complacency and boredom with the topic is the enemy that causes accidents. When your title encapsulates what you are going to say, all the better.

*Freakonomics* is the name of the best-seller written by economist Steven D. Levitt and journalist Stephen J. Dubner. Readers are divided, as they often are when it's a new approach, thinking it's either brilliant or just silly. (Not surprisingly, many of the critics are economists and other academics.)

The title itself is arresting, but so are the chapter headings, especially in the sequel, *Superfreakonomics*.* Try these:

How is a street prostitute like a department store Santa?

and

Why should suicide bombers buy life insurance?

I won't be a spoiler and tell you the answers; it's hard not to be intrigued.

Queen's 'Bohemian Rhapsody' is a notable exception to the musical rule that some part of the title should be in the chorus. The words 'Bohemian' and 'Rhapsody' appear nowhere in the

---

* Stephen J. Dubner and Steven D. Levitt, *Superfreakonomics* (2010).

song. Just as well – they're hard to sing, even harder to rhyme. The number also plays around somewhat with the traditional verse-chorus structure, to the extent that I miss the old format terribly. So if you choose a really bizarre title, you'd better give a great talk!

## The joy of names

'Eleanor Rigby', 'Strawberry Fields Forever', 'Lucy in the Sky with Diamonds' and 'I Am the Walrus' are intriguing. As the Beatles became bolder and more ambitious with their titles, they morphed from a skiffle and R & B covers group into the world's house band.

These titles work because they conjure up a picture. Maybe a different picture for individual listeners, but a picture all the same. Listening to music is like seeing faces in the clouds or shapes in a fire. We individually construct and are gripped by the images we see, which may or may not overlap with our neighbour's perception. A striking name or title makes it more easy to have a common, shared picture in the mind. Choose the concrete over the abstract.

A fascination with words extends to an interest in names and titles. One of my favourite band names is I Love You ... But I've Chosen Darkness. It's a quintet from Texas (and they're quite good).

Or for a great song title there's Canadian band Woodpigeon's 'In The Battle of Sun vs Curtains, Sun Loses and We Sleep Until Noon'. (It's a great tune, too!) Even more bizarrely, there's a Swedish band called Ghost, in which every band member is called 'Nameless Ghoul'. An interesting problem to have when it comes to booking a restaurant, I imagine.

I'm fascinated by the freshness brought to English by people for whom it's a second language. I love the title of Danish band Mew's song: 'Am I Wry? No!' Or Norwegian lo-fi act Kings of Convenience's album title: *Quiet Is The New Loud.*

Whatever you choose, make sure it intrigues your audience *and* encapsulates the theme. Naming matters.

## Use Golden Facts

How many people were killed or injured by wolves in America last year? Three hundred? A thousand? Hold that thought for a minute ...

It's easy to mistake facts for knowledge or wisdom in the age of information overload. Much of what we hear is opinion, or context-dependent. A survey may show that 33 per cent of Texans believe in alien abduction, but is that really a fact? Given the human tendency to extrapolate, it soon will be! A little sleight of mind is all it takes for this survey's findings to morph into 'most Americans believe' and even 'a significant proportion of people in the civilised world actually think ...' and so on.

I call this 'fallacy inflation'.

You should banish these kinds of factoids from your talk. They are about as accurate as the Katie Melua song title, 'Nine Million Bicycles (in Beijing)'. (Although that at least conjures a powerful image and has some poetry to it.) A survey tells you only what the survey tells you – but superstitiously we believe in them. They are like the fairy tales of the so-called rational age.

On the other hand, there are universal 'facts'. What happens when two chemical compounds are mixed, or the mathematical equations for working out the tensile strength of a bridge, will be true in Karachi or Cape Town. Although even here the interpretation of these facts may not be identical: as psychologist Carl Jung remarked, everything we 'know' has a penumbra of uncertainty about it. I've never managed to get that line into a business talk.

---

**Prove It – with Facts!**

Comedian Stewart Lee describes having an argument with a taxi driver in London on the subject of immigration. The discussion terminated when the driver said, 'Well, you can prove anything with **facts**!'

I've been trying to use this in a debate ever since.

---

Golden facts are ones that embody some bigger truth, stick in the mind and have some rigour behind them – so surveys are usually out. The facts you want to use should illuminate your topic, providing a hook for the wider concept you are explaining.

George Monbiot is a highly articulate and passionate environmentalist. I attended a talk he gave on 'wilding the environment', particularly the research on the benefits of reintroducing wolves. Surprisingly, this improves biodiversity: prey like deer stay away from exposed riverbanks where plants and trees can then flourish, and so on.

Sounds admirable? However, in many countries there is a deep-rooted prejudice against the wolf, doubtless fed by countless movies in which they howl fiendishly through the night, and eventually eat the intrepid hunter.*

In his talks, Monbiot encapsulates the irrationality of this lupine fear by an illuminating fact: **no** people were killed or injured by wolves (at least in 2013). Fair enough, but here's his punchline: seventeen were killed in incidents with … vending machines!

## Facts that make you think

The authors of *Freakonomics* are great at using facts to explore counterintuitive truths. While many Americans don't want

---

* The full argument is more complex and beyond the remit of *RYP*. Monbiot's book is *Feral: Rewilding the Land, Sea and Human Life* (2014).

their kids to play at the homes of families who possess firearms, the chances of their children drowning in their neighbour's swimming pool are actually many times greater than the likelihood of being killed by a gun. The odds of death by pool are 1 in 11,000; by gun, 1 death for every 1 million guns.

After 9/11, some people were understandably put off flying. In a terrible example of the law of unintended consequences, this put thousands more cars on the roads, leading to hundreds of extra deaths. The *facts* tell us flying is safer, but fear is stronger.

Behind all these examples is an attempt to make people think beyond the obvious. The facts, like stories, must have some insight, point or relevance embodied in them.

Sometimes the facts themselves *are* the stories.

Ask most people in the USA what they think of the current crime rate, and they will shake their heads sadly. Of course, there are still far too many tragic incidents, but if you look coolly at the statistics, serious crime has nose-dived to 1970s levels. We are so used to the 'fact' of crime rates worsening that we don't even see the decline, even when the cold evidence tells us it's happening.

One scientist who *did* notice trends shifting towards the positive is renowned Harvard Professor Steven Pinker, famous for his many books on the brain and language. His 2011 opus, *The Better Angels of Our Nature**\* describes, with the actual figures calmly noted, how over the last fifty years the world has become safer, healthier, more crime-free and richer, even in Africa. Whether you look at death in childbirth, cancer survival rates, longevity, GDP, whatever, the graph of improvement curves ever upward.

Now this doesn't mean for one minute that everything is swell on Planet Earth: serious challenges like climate change

---

\* Steven Pinker, *The Better Angels of Our Nature* (2011).

have the potential to reverse all the good we've achieved in recent decades.

But what we *believe* to be the facts is often irrational, and so it's important to be more thoughtful – and sceptical – about what the facts really are, and what they mean.

Just make sure that the fascinating and striking examples you use have a point, answering the simple objection in the audience's mind: 'Why is that relevant?' Perhaps the taxi driver was right after all: you *can* prove anything with facts.

## The Power Chords of Speaking: Things to think and do

◄◄ Think back to the stories you've actually remembered from talks in the past. What hooked you? How were they delivered? Think of a scene-setting tale that encodes your theme, or a personal one that underscores your passion for it.

▌▌ Decide where in your presentation the stories fit.

▶ BUILD A GARAGE! Turn two of your concepts or phrases into a word picture, a visual image.

▶ Read some quality 'lyrics' or prose – say, in the *New Yorker* or the *London Review of Books*. Note some of the fresh words, phrases or neologisms you've picked up.

▶ Give your talk and its subsections 'sexier' and stronger titles.

▌▌ Research left-field but striking data – or 'golden facts' – that illuminate your topic.

## The Power Chords of Speaking: Your notes

# PART II

# Rocking your audience

# SOUND AND VISION –

## A Punk Guide to *Life* by PowerPoint

- ◆ Find Your Voice
- ◆ *Life* by PowerPoint
- ◆ The Power of Props
- ◆ Going Unplugged – Why Lo-Fi Can Work

I'm writing this at a European Education Summit where I'm due to speak later in the day. It's a fascinating event where teachers are sharing collaborative methods of learning fuelled by new digital technology. Using iPads and an array of intuitive software, students effectively create their own textbooks, learning timetables and content using video, music and graphics that would have been unimaginable less than a decade ago.

So in the era of the screenager when everyone can be their own Spielberg or David Lynch, why would anyone listen to a stick figure on a stage? Aren't words and PowerPoint like the talk and chalk of our forefathers?

It's a classic case of both-and. While the classroom is being revolutionised and learners become digital citizens, there's simultaneously a boom in attendance at live lectures, philosophy boot camps, literary festivals, intellectual debates (like Hitchens vs Galloway) and the flagship for clever exposition, TED Talks.

Clearly, videos, voting pads, live Twitter feeds and apps can enrich interaction and learning. But if you have something to say, remember that an *audi*-ence is not an accidental label for those listening to you. They want to hear or 'audio' you first, see you second. Good visuals help, but they can't make poor language great, any more than a good video can turn a middle-of-the-road song into great music. We'll cover both voice and visuals here.

We'll also explore how props can be useful. Then we'll finish on an alternative approach: going 'unplugged' is the lo-fi delivery that can sometimes reach an audience better than a slick, hi-tech presentation or pitch.

Why a punk guide? I have to admit I wouldn't normally choose to listen to much of that music today, but the brief spasm of punk in its heyday did at least shake up the old order, the overblown excesses of prog rock and performances in huge arenas. Punk is rock's awkward, bastard cousin. It's visceral, in your face, makes you move and bonds performer and audience in a pummelling embrace. 'Anyone can play guitar' was the motto of the day. You can use punk's energy and directness – spitting and body piercing is optional.

◆

## Find Your Voice

Monotonous is onomatopoeic. It sounds like its meaning – monotonous. For people's minds to tune in – and stay tuned – you need to vary your speech patterns, or their reptilian brains will take over. Perceiving no variation in the environment, they will fall asleep and bask in the warm, safe sunshine of your flat delivery. It's why there's a middle eight in a popular song: listeners are getting bored with the predictability and need something new to engage them. It's the same with your audience.

Your voice is your voice, and there's only a certain amount you can change through professional voice training: breathing, enunciation, projection and so on. These courses are valuable, but you're probably not going take them, are you? So here's the punk shortcut. Just like anyone can play guitar, anyone can learn fairly quickly to improve their voice more swiftly than the experts would have you believe.

Invoking the spirit of the Sex Pistol's album *Never Mind the Bollocks*, you can quickly improve your voice's:

- Volume

- Tempo

- Clarity

- Tone

## Volume

Volume has a three-note structure: loud, conversational and whispered. Practise these modes of speaking into a tape recorder or your smartphone; listen and reflect. Which passages of your talk are appropriate for which volume level?

You shouldn't need to go up to eleven in volume, especially if you're using a microphone, but it's good to see what it sounds like. Save it for picking up new themes, emphasis or punchlines to stories.

The opposite of dialling up is *sotto voce* remarks. Strangely they can emphasise your points in a powerful way. An observant listener from Standard Chartered Bank pointed out that when I was speaking I often showed my true feelings in these asides, which he likened to the utterances of Shakespeare's fools. A fool's apparently sarcastic or flippant lines often contain the wisdom of a savant in the guise of an idiot.

Now I'm not saying that my asides had the same wisdom or literary merit as the Bard's, but this feedback made me think about the subtle power of expressing ideas at this less noisy, more intimate volume.

Tom Peters, co-author of best-selling *In Search of Excellence* and passionate speaker, is a master of the resigned aside, usually reserved for contempt at arrogance or complacency. He's almost muttering to himself, but it's very much meant for broadcast. You sense he's sharing his inner frustrations with you in these quieter moments, and you listen harder.

A microphone is the wonderful technology that allows you, paradoxically, to become more intimate with the group. The audience's fear of the microphone is one you need to conquer if you want them to use it to respond. All too often they will look at it as if it's a bomb or alien technology, declaring, 'I don't think I need it.'

Well, if *you* do, then they definitely do. The blind spot is that we only hear our own voice reverberating inside our skull, and can be clueless about the volume needed to be heard. People hold hand-held mikes either too close or too far away from their mouth. The best tip is to tell them it's an ice cream, and they should imagine they are licking it.

The unamplified voice has a natural timbre to it that we'd all prefer, but if you're ever in doubt whether to use a mike or not, then *do*. A voice that is on the edge of audibility strains the listener. And if you are straining to project your voice, the effect is the same on you.

## Tempo

The tempo at which you speak also makes a big difference. We all know that if we're nervous, we tend to gabble, and if we're speaking publicly, the chances of doing this are greatly increased. Motormouths suck the oxygen out of the room. As business and educational presenter Brian Weller says, 'Syntax eats up $CO_2$!'

But just 'knowing' this doesn't stop most speakers from going too fast, especially as the clock runs down and we feel the need to 'cover' all the points.

Muddy Waters can teach us how to slow down. Waters described himself as a 'delay singer': his voice would come in a little later than the beat. The effect is transfixing – while a nervous singer will come in ahead of the beat, and all Eurovision pop is jauntily *on* the beat, many of the greats just hang back a little. The great Nick Drake often did this.

Guitarist and musicologist Bob Brozman observes that the music of the coloniser is *on* the beat – it's martial – whereas that of many colonised peoples is *off* the beat. My own speaking 'beat' tends to be one-two: theory (one); practice (two); a model (one); its practical application (two); a provocative thought (one); then a 'so what?' (two).

What's your beat?

Ask others to let you know if it's not clear to you. It took me some time to recognise what I was doing semi-consciously, which allowed me to make it a more precise part of my speaking rhythm.

You don't need to know Muddy Waters's music (though listening to 'Mannish Boy' surely can't do any harm) to have an instant mnemonic here to use while speaking. Whenever I sense I'm throwing ideas too fast in the face of the crowd, I think 'Muddy Waters'. It creates a useful pause and makes me take it a little slower – which is usually more effective.

Holding back a little is a powerful ingredient for producing intensity in your voice and tension in your delivery. Peter Green, arguably the best white blues guitarist, was brilliant at this. Listen to 'A Love that Burns', and you'll gain inspiration from the way he delays his guitar break. When the lead solo eventually comes in, it's all the more memorable for his earlier restraint.

**Telephone Number Speed**

Have you noticed how quickly someone speaks when leaving their own telephone number on your voicemail? They know it, so why don't you?

This is a powerful analogy for the speed **not** to speak at in a talk. Think of 'chunking' the information – the area code is one chunk (then pause), the next two sections of numbers are similarly chunks you need to pause between.

Remember 'telephone numbers' occasionally when you're speaking, and it may help you to slow down a little, and chunk your information so the listener can take it in.

The message is clear – be more like a delay singer than a chatterbox when you are presenting. Your pace should usually be this: *slower than you think!* And pause more often. This simple punk advice can immediately improve your delivery.

Second language audiences need special care, and it's often the kind of group I'm speaking to. Early on, I do a **speed and clarity check**, agreeing with a volunteer in the audience sign language she will give me if I'm going too fast or not making sense. Usually she will need to flag me down at least once. This helps a great deal in tuning yourself in to the listener's rhythm and speed of understanding.

Logical? Yes, I hope so – but logic doesn't always help us change. To make this point more effectively, I recommend listening to Michael Jackson's great dance hit, 'Billie Jean', followed by a recent acoustic version by American artists the Civil Wars. Theirs is live, and a contender for best ever cover song. The harmonies of the male and female voice are gorgeous, but most of all 'Billie Jean' is transformed by the m u c h  s l o w e r  t e m p o.

I ask the speaker I'm coaching to do a passage of their talk at Michael Jackson speed, and then the Civil Wars tempo. It's a simple way of remembering what's fast and upbeat, what's slower and intense. Naturally, you may use either tempo for different material: now you have a simple punk two-chord reminder.

## Clarity

Clarity has two aspects: the way you express an idea, and your speech patterns. One of the politician's favourite phrases is, 'Let me be perfectly clear', when they are being anything but.

To be clear within your own head is one thing; conveying it to another is something else. Rehearse out loud and take it at the audience's comprehension speed. It's probably slower than your own – not because they are stupid, but because it's the first time they have heard the material and are busy processing. And not merely processing: they are also having an internal dialogue with themselves, a phenomenon colleague Mark Brown calls 'head chatter'. Your pauses and relaunches into your material will help to cut through at least some of this internal dialogue.

The clarity of your speech *patterns* will similarly be helped greatly by eliminating – or at least reducing – interference from 'ums', 'ers', 'you knows' and other verbal tics that distract. These phrases and mannerisms are often invisible to the speaker, which is why I recommend trying it out on another, even if it's someone who doesn't understand the subject matter.

In fact, *especially* if they don't know the topic.

When you can explain something clearly to an intelligent listener with zero background in your field, you're on the way to greater clarity. Above all because you will need to put your thoughts *into context*. Why is this relevant? What's the point of it? How does it link to other aspects of the topic?

## Tone

Tone is almost as important as your content: it's the key to tuning in to or alienating your audience. The tone of many sales conferences segues between pop and heavy metal, while school lessons are all too often like elevator music, a vague drone in the background that doesn't disturb the students' reverie or texting too much.

One musical definition of a tone is the timbre of an instrument. A guitar or violin is distinct from a piano, even if it's playing the same notes. Here the instrument is your voice.

Should your tone be:

- Conversational or declamatory?
- Intimate or challenging?
- Formal or informal?
- In your face or elliptical?

Adventurer and speaker Matt Dickinson is a master at varying his tone. I've seen him deliver essentially the same talk to an audience of business executives and a group of teenagers. (He's also a successful writer of teen fiction.) The older group could tolerate more abstractions about commitment, endurance and leadership, whereas the intelligent young audience tuned in more to the weird practicalities of eating and eliminating at altitude.

It wasn't an adult who asked the question about what happens to your pee at sub-zero temperatures. Answer: it freezes before it hits the ground. Also details of why Matt took fifty energy bars (and ate them within a week), and how to boil water on Everest, engaged the teenagers greatly. Most importantly, at no time did you feel he was patronising them – he was tuning in to what grabbed them the most.

When I'm doing conference design, I often ask the customer to think about their event in terms of musical genres.

Do they want their meeting to feel like:

- **Folk**. An intimate, largely 'unplugged' chat by the fireside

or

- **Cool Jazz**. Lots of improvisation and risk-taking

or

- **Rock**. High energy, music, lights, videos, audience involvement

or

- **Classical**. Perfectly orchestrated with choral (group interaction) sessions, motifs interwoven and brought together in a great crescendo

or

- **Indie or Punk**. Getting down and dirty to discuss challenges in quick, punchy bursts. Everyone involved!

The question frequently triggers a creative line of thought about the style or feel of the event. Often it's a genre-crossing mix of styles that's needed, and it's very useful to have a language or shorthand for something that's essentially inde-finable, yet vital to get right.

## Life *by PowerPoint*

There's been a strong reaction to the misuse and overuse of PowerPoint – or Keynote, or other formats of showing slides and visuals. At times, it's an *over*reaction. I've been to events where the 'no PowerPoint' rule meant that lovely, pastoral ani-mations drifted across screens, with little or no connection to the messages the speakers were trying to communicate. I felt almost nostalgic for bullet points.

Speaking to a small group is something I enjoy doing without PowerPoint. I'm in good company – Harvard Business School professors to this day use chalk on green boards, and are very good at it! But for a group of more than, say, twenty-five, it helps to have engaging visual support for your words.

When I'm asked *not* to use PowerPoint, it's because of an understandable fear of that old headache, Death by PowerPoint. My response tends to be that I'll be doing Life by PowerPoint, and usually I've won the client over after I've spoken. This section and the next is about how to achieve this.

## You are not your slides

Naturally, *you* are the prime visual – how you move, what you do with your body to emphasise a point, express emotion or connect with your audience.

You are in the foreground; your images, pictures, Power-Point, Keynote or whatever you use is the backing band.

Why is this so key? Presenters talk about their 'deck' of slides, and in some institutions teachers deliver another's deck! More energy can be spent getting the animations right than creating the content. Look – if you can tell what a speaker's going to say from their slides, the slides are rubbish! Content like this could be on a handout or available online. The punk guide is simple and direct:

- Visuals should be ... visual.
- Visuals should be striking, fascinating, funny, provocative and memorable.
- Lists are out, and
- You are *not* your slides (again).

You can tell if a speaker is overshadowed by their own slides: they are half-turned towards the next visual, their minds immersed in *it* and absent from *you*, the audience.

Attention is the greatest gift a musician or speaker can give – you know with your survivalist, crocodile brain, whether someone has their attention on you or not. You can't have your mind on your slides *and* your audience. Maybe you can multitask in life, but it's hard to do so when you're teaching or presenting ideas. The same goes for your audience: are they meant to be listening to you, or looking at your slides? Especially if these are crammed with words and numbers.

At bigger events you may have 'comfort monitors', plasma screens with your slides and, if needed, text on them – the closest most of us come to having an autocue. This makes sense, especially the version which allows you, but not the audience, to see your *next* slide. The received wisdom is that you should not read your own slides, and this technology allows you to at least *appear* not to be doing so.

However, this advice, like most popular tips about presenting, needs challenging. Your image may have a punchline or a surprise on it – if so, you absolutely *should* sometimes move into the audience, look at the screen and share the experience with them. It's analogous to the music performer leaping into the crowd. Too much of it is disruptive; a little breaks that invisible screen between performer and listener.

## Less is more

Another way to live the philosophy of 'I am not my slides' is simply to have fewer of them. Often I have to savage a speaker's forty-slide talk that's meant to magically fit into a twelve-minute speaking slot. This becomes a race against the clock which stresses the speaker, and gives the crowd a headache. The only rule of thumb for how many visuals you should have is:

*Fewer than you think.*

Actually, that's easy listening advice. It should be:

*Far, far fewer than you think!*

This rule holds whether you're describing dissipative structures in chemistry, the Dissolution of the Monasteries, or a new agenda for sustainability. *If in doubt, cut it out.* I go through several, or even many, iterations of a talk, considering each image and whether it earns its place. Any doubt, and it's out! Catch yourself thinking, 'Well, it's safer if I include it', and you're like the Linus character in Charlie Brown cartoons, clinging on to his blanket for comfort.

OK. If pressed, I'll give you a number from my field, business speaking. Twenty images is *possible* for an hour of speaking. But ten to fifteen is much better. Some to dwell on, some to move through more quickly. Lists, tables, examples and explanatory detail can be on handouts, though preferably leave this to the end for the gannets who still collect paper. (Web links are more useful.)

## Mental interaction

Above all, to avoid Death by PowerPoint, make some of your images *mentally interactive*. I call this 'instrumental'. Instead of a flat, on-the-screen, passive viewing process, use punchlines and quizzes.

I love the humour and ingenuity of the south London firm of Indian plumbers, Patel & Patel. Their advertisement goes like this:

You've tried the Cowboys

Then builds:

Now try the Indians!

This seems obvious, but all too often I've seen speakers blow it by showing the whole text or image. As with this quote from English retail supremo Sir Philip Green:

Unsuccessful companies have meetings.

Then ...

Successful ones have parties.

Simply by building up the picture or theme together, you tune in more to the listener's rhythm.

Do you have graphs to build up? Get the audience to guess trends and figures. Put in some twists like a line that shows how you *thought* they'd guess – only then reveal the actual trend or figure. Artfully hand-drawn graphs can be more appealing than traditional PowerPoint templates.

Simple quizzes keep the crowd more awake. Suppose you want to tell them that a large percentage of sales people in the USA failed to successfully pitch what was better or different about their product, when compared with a cheaper competitor version.

The trick is to give the audience alternatives, either to shout out, or to click on a voting app.* Give them four possible answers:

* Voting apps are increasingly a part of conference life. They can be useful in gathering data, even if it's gut responses, in the moment. But don't mistake it for real interaction – typing in a number is no substitute for thought.

- 56 per cent
- 68 per cent
- 83 per cent
- 99 per cent

The value of a voting device is not so much the percentages that appear on the screen, but the discussion you facilitate afterwards about why so many got it right or wrong.

There's a great deal more complexity that can be used in eliciting responses from a quiz: your guiding principle should be to get people to *experience* the steps of your argument.

Build in interaction with your visuals and your ideas will lodge more readily in the mind. Whenever you can, choose an active approach over a passive one. This is what I mean by 'instrumental': the interaction is in people's minds. They may not be speaking out loud – nevertheless they are busy making the connections you want between the neurons of their brains.

Videos are thought to 'raise the energy' in a presentation. This is only true if they are short and funny. Otherwise they trigger the TV couch potato response in the room. The most effective ones are not usually the slick, for-broadcast types, but homemade ones, 'vox pop' of your audience or students, especially ones created in the moment. The new digital technology means we can all create moving images complete with titles and music, which may have more power than something lifted from YouTube,* which anyone could have found in their lunch break.

---

* The legality of what you can and cannot show is sometimes grey, and doubtless will have changed with new technologies by the time you read this. Check who the owner is and what their standard terms and conditions for use are.

## Life by PowerPoint – top 10

I've worked with some of the world's best event production teams. They create powerful visuals and branding for demanding business clients, professional pitches and internal conferences around the world. In discussions at a number of events, I teased out their top ten principles for creating effective visuals.

1.  **Images** – striking, beautiful and not obvious. Search well for alternatives.

2.  **Fonts** – at least two sizes larger than you think. What looks big enough on your PC won't be on a conference screen.

3.  **Builds** – don't overdo them. They take the brain away from focusing on your delivery. Save them for punchlines.

4.  **Cartoons** – don't! (Unless they are from someone great like Gary Larson – and you'll have to pay a royalty.)

5.  **Lengthy definitions and quotes** – just don't. You can memorise or read them – only put the essence on your slides.

6.  **Bullet points** – only if you *really* have to (and you don't, do you? They are just to organise your own mind). The audience won't really pay attention to them anyway.

7.  **Words** – as few as possible.

8.  **Graphs/histograms/picture diagrams** – as simple as you can. Then simplify again. This is where you almost **must** use builds.

9. **Gimmicks** – (clever fades, dissolves and whooshing sound effects) if you must.

10. **Less is** definitely **more** – less information, fewer slides, less text, less everything.

Paul 'Chubby' Evans is the event manager for Partytecture, putting on conferences around the world for many of the most demanding corporations. He has sat through literally thousands of presentations around the globe in the last ten years. He says:

> ❝ If you just read the bullet points, then why bother – the audience could have done that without you. Only use technology if it actually supports and enhances your message. If you are talking about a topic that needs complicated charts, make sure your can see and understand your visuals at a glance. Always have ready an emailable set of shareable content and tell the audience that you will share this content with them. While the audience is looking at the detail on the screen, they are not engaging with you. If you have a two-minute videotape that has an interesting twenty seconds in it, just show the twenty seconds. ❞

Whenever you hear a presenter say, 'I hope you can see this in the back row', it means that even those in the front row need hawk-like vision to read it. Get off the stage and see what your visuals look like from the back of the room. A bit of respect for the audience's point of view is all it takes.

## Beyond bullet points

Visuals should be ... visual. It sounds *so* obvious, but I see this simple advice being ignored all the time.

Bullet points are out. Lengthy quotes are out. Overloaded graphs are definitely out. Complex strategic matrices should never have been considered in the first place.

Which leaves us with: pictures, pithy statements or short quotes, simple graphs and videos. Plenty to work with!

iStockphoto and Shutterstock are great sources of images you can purchase fairly cheaply, and under certain conditions use professionally. Wherever you find your images – today we all carry cameras with us, so you may have created your own – try to use ones that are not obvious, clichéd depictions of say, Albert Einstein or Gandhi. You might find a computer-generated image with an impressionistic likeness of the great scientist, or a picture of a huge crowd of Indians sitting on a beach waiting for the Mahatma.

Intriguing works as well, if your image is a bit left field, or there's an illuminating story related to it.

### Surprising Slides

My criterion for an interesting set of slides is that you shouldn't be able to tell what's going to be said just by looking at them. You will pick up some highlights, but most of all you'll get the 'tone' or 'feel' of the talk. What brings it alive, gives it a clear narrative and aliveness of expression is you.

The slides are your servant, not your equal or master.

## Beyond PowerPoint

We're using 'PowerPoint' as a shorthand for slides here, though Keynote is, as you'd expect, a little cooler. A rocked-up analysis by Robert Simpson on the blog Orbiting Frog goes: 'Keynote wears sunglasses, smokes roll-ups and was making slides before it was cool.'

You might find the ubiquity of PowerPoint more convenient, though. At business events, you're less likely to have any compatibility problems.

PowerPoint and Keynote aren't the only visual systems. One newcomer is Prezi, which calls itself a 'zoomable' technology. This allows you to start with a page, rather like a mind map, a canvas on which you can zoom and drill down into chosen areas. In theory, this allows you to show the relationships between the big picture and fine detail. You can navigate between video, text and images, so clearly Prezi has the potential to be more entertaining and arresting than the linear sequence of PowerPoint.

I've seen it used well and badly: you're certainly going to have to invest some time getting familiar with the tool if you want to give a fluent presentation, where the cleverness of the show doesn't draw all the attention away from you.

Prezi can come into its own in a pitch situation. A colleague was pitching for some consultancy business and divided the home page of his Prezi talk into these topics presented as icons:

- About us
- About you
- Your challenges
- The solutions
- Research we've done
- Executive summary

The listeners were then invited to say what topic they'd like to hear about *first*. Prezi allows you to zoom over to one of these icons and immediately go into a more three-dimensional, visual representation of your ideas. You couldn't do this very easily with the more traditional slide technologies: there would be a lot of annoying scrolling going on, as well as not having the Prezi ability to zoom across and open up a fresh world of possibilities.

Naturally you need to be very well rehearsed to run a conversation like this. The trick is to work out your links on to the next area, especially if the pitchee is cheeky and asks to see your solutions first! It's riskier, but can be more engaging than the plodding nature of Slide 1, Slide 2, Slide 3, etc.

My problem with Prezi is that the technology can distract from the message. I suspect that in a few years we'll all be more familiar with acting like a one-person video production team – that's what it feels like – and so the advantages will outweigh the downsides. It's worth exploring, but don't let it take you over.

PechaKucha is another approach. This time it's not so much the technology as the format: twenty slides, which automatically advance after twenty seconds. PechaKucha nights are held in over seven hundred cities worldwide, which means it's a very democratic process. Even five-year-olds have told their story in this way.

You could certainly try a PechaKucha sequence for a part of your talk, or as a rehearsal tool for making sure your speech is succinct and visual. For a half-hour talk, it could get rather wearing; again, too much attention on the images, not enough on the speaker.

I can't leave the subject of striking visuals without mentioning two bibles on the subject, which will expand your thinking about what's possible. *Presentation Zen* by Garr Reynolds describes practically and psychologically how to use slides which are less cluttered, more beautiful and effective. It's perhaps the only book where the introduction is in PowerPoint – lean, crisp and to the point.

*Information Is Beautiful* by David McCandless ups the game even further. Presenting results of research from the very specific – like the world's favourite drinks and hangover cures – to broader topics like carbon emissions, designer McCandless uses fine and original art to bring the results alive. What lies flat on the page in numbers and words is brought to almost holographic life with skill and wit. You may not be able to reproduce these, but they will make you reconsider how to make data live and breathe. And, yes, some of McCandless's images *are* beautiful.

## The Power of Props

Props help to make your content multi-sensory, three-dimensional, as distinct from the flatland of thoughts and slides. It's where science has an advantage: passing around a human brain, participating in a practical experiment or holding an engineered component all help to bring theory to life.

Bruce Dickinson, lead singer of Iron Maiden, professional pilot and aeronautical entrepreneur, is a remarkable man. I was interviewing him in front of an audience, and I had proposed that he brought along something physical, in part to counteract any disappointment that he wasn't actually going to sing. He came to the event with a theremin and left it on the stage throughout the interview.

The theremin is a strange and wonderful musical instrument: it's played without being touched. Leon Theremin patented the device in 1928. By moving hand or body near the two antennae – one for pitch, the other volume – signals are amplified and channelled through a loudspeaker. The sounds it makes just by waving your hand or moving your

body near it are extraordinarily tuneful, alien-sounding woo-
woo noises.*

At the end of the session, numerous people came up to play
with it, chatting to Bruce about his fascination with the instrument. He's passionate about engineering and innovation, and
this became an enjoyable coda to the session as he talked about
Theremin's history.

To sound and vision you can also add the sense of touch.
Feeling and holding an item – especially if it's one that actually
does something, like the theremin – helps to give body, weight
and memorability to your topic. You are making the intangible,
tangible.

## Simple props

Props don't need to be sophisticated to make a point. I've used
the humble coat hanger to spark a debate about awareness of
the customer's needs. For me, a hotel which cannot be bothered
to give you proper hanging devices for your clothes – in case
you walk off with a few pennies worth of their property – is
going to fall down in other areas of service. It's a Van Halen
moment.

Brandishing a coat hanger stolen from my room – either
a proper one or the fiddly type – I ask the group to consider
their own 'coat hanger moments': the things that seem small
from inside the organisation, but are real annoyances seen
from the customer's point of view. It's a tremendous eye-
opener, especially because so many of these barriers between
you and your customer can be fixed once you see them.
People remember the idea of 'coat hanger moments' rather
better than any exhortation to 'see the world through your
customer's eyes'.

* Theremin would probably have been a fan of the wonderfully strange band
Portishead.

What visual and tangible mnemonics can you bring along? For a serious speaker on a serious topic, this might seem like child's play. Well, that's exactly what it is, a grown-up version of show and tell, a practical application of Einstein's remark that creativity is 'serious play'.

Thom Brown is legendary in Hewlett Packard Printing for his use of props and role plays that make his points memorable. He describes himself as an 'inkologist', but also claims to make the world's best margaritas.

He invites people on stage to test his perfect brew, and then encourages them to mix up a cheap version which uses happy hour cheap tequila, powdered lime and sweet n low instead of his agave nectar and fresh limes. The result is almost undrinkable, which gives Thom his segue into the science of inferior printing ink compared with the quality HP variety. Graphically he brings home the message of why a better ink costs more, but may be the best option.

Delegates I've talked to remember this years later. They've forgotten everything else that was said at that event, but still recall Thom's talk.

### Al Gore's Ladder

In his talk for the film *An Inconvenient Truth*, Al Gore visually reinforces the notion of climate change running away with us by climbing a ladder. He does this to graphically represent that the negative indicators are going up and beyond his screen. It's corny, but effective. Anything that helps you 'think out of the screen' is going to make your argument more engaging.

## *You* as a prop

Don't lose sight of the fact that the best 'prop' is you. So put on your red shoes. That's just what an immaculately dressed business colleague does (he has three pairs of red, Puma Ferrari shoes). He believes that this gives the audience a visual memory aid, reinforcing in a small way his message of thinking differently. They certainly remember him.

Don't be distracting with how you dress: step in front of a group in a purple jumpsuit and you'll be remembered for all the wrong reasons. One unusual detail in how you dress is often enough; give the audience something interesting to focus on, and in a small way their attention is drawn to you.

Now, how superficial can you get? We have become a race that expects more visual stimulation than in the past. Video didn't just kill the radio star – it took over our minds.

My daughter put it rather well,* speaking at her coming-of-age party:

> ❝My grandparents grew up in black and white, my parents in colour. My generation is growing up in 3D!❞

My long-suffering colleague Robert Maguire started a presentation in Italy dressed in a Viking helmet (to introduce the serious theme of selling value – what it takes to be a 'Value Warrior'). He also appeared on stage in Hamburg wearing a crocodile's head to highlight the notion of aggressive purchasing strategies used against the sales people in the audience.†

Props work, provided you link the visual to the verbal, using the object as a way of summarising or introducing your theme.

---

* Of course, I'm wildly biased!
† Robert – thank you for doing this with such good humour.

## *Going Unplugged – Why Lo-Fi Can Work*

As the kings of electrified grunge rock, it's fascinating to hear a nervous but on-form Kurt Cobain when Nirvana played a live *MTV Unplugged* set in New York in 1993. There's something about the rawness of this semi-acoustic set that really touches you, even though he is clearly stretching the limits of his voice.

What's striking is the contrast between the well-known image of the heavy, electric Nirvana and this lighter, unplugged performance: somehow the dissonance makes their 'naked' appearance more riveting.

When you need to transmit an idea, how much of it can you put over with lo-fi technology, and can you whisper rather than shout? This could relate to corporate communications, an advertising campaign ... whatever. Often being slick or loud gets between you and your audience, and the last place you want this distance is in a professional pitch situation.

Seeing singer-songwriter Ryan Adams perform acoustically is a revelation. Even though, like Nick Drake, he loves to play on a temperamental and battered old guitar. 'Now you can actually hear me,' he explains between songs, 'instead of my voice being drowned in reverb.'* He captures very well the difference between his loud, electric performances and his more intimate acoustic ones.

What is the 'reverb' that drowns the clarity and directness of your presentation? And how do you make your communications more immediate and designed for human ears? In other words, how do you go 'unplugged'?

## Technology meltdown

Sometimes it's technology meltdown that forces you to go acoustic. Here's what happened to me, fortuitously, as it turned out.

* Concert in Oxford, UK, in 2013. For me, Adams was also the standout performance at the world's most revered rock festival, Glastonbury, in 2015.

I'm frozen on stage, somewhere in Europe, with 150 managers of a well-known company waiting expectantly for me to begin. Murphy's imp is having a field day: minutes before I'm introduced, the event organiser whispers that instead of the allotted hour, I have only forty minutes. Why? Because the morning had overrun and the CEO had had to do his slot on time so he could come in, press some flesh and leave for a flight. In this business, invoking the name of the CEO had a small whiff of 'Dear Leader' about it. I complied.

Now that would have been manageable; I quickly decided the passages I was going to leave out. But the compère now managed to fluff his introduction, announcing the title of my talk incorrectly. He also used a couple of lines I normally use to introduce myself.

When my opening slide came up, I noticed that it was the wrong presentation, the one I thought I'd buried last night. Not wanting my first words to be, 'these are the wrong slides' (tantamount to saying 'I'm an imposter') I signalled to the AV team to change them. Unfortunately we hadn't worked out our body language signs, so his desktop appeared on the main conference screen as he scrolled through his PowerPoint library. Some great holiday snaps, but he couldn't find the new set of slides.

By now I had been introduced, was standing on stage and the expectant glow that follows initial applause had faded into awkward silence. People were starting to do that very twenty-first-century thing when a small window of opportunity opens: checking their mobiles. And did I mention that this was the after-lunch session?

So let's leave me frozen there for a minute. What would you do, or have you done, when all your planning and careful preparation is in meltdown? When I've asked this question to people I've been coaching to present, I've been struck by how often they fall back on metaphors from fields they feel at home with. For instance, if sport is your passion, you may find yourself thinking or saying something like, 'When the going gets tough'. If it's history, you may dig into your memory for a Churchillian quote – 'We will never surrender.'

This might sound a little over the top as a response to a situation where nobody's going to die – or even lose their job. But tell that to someone who is standing in front of a roomful of busy people, high on expectation and low on tolerance. There's something about the very public nature of this potential humiliation that can frighten even the most experienced speaker.

The default setting in my brain is music, so that's where I went for help. As I stood there, smiling positively but not feeling it, a phrase came into my mind:

'Ladies and gentlemen, let's do this unplugged.' It wasn't very effective in calling the group away from the joys of texting or chatting with their neighbour. They looked bemused, and my next crack about 'technology is the name we give to something that doesn't quite work ... yet' wasn't appreciated – this was, after all, a company with a heavy presence in the technology sector.

## Go acoustic

If in doubt, act, I thought. So I jumped off the stage. It was a bit higher than I thought. Still, no bones broken. I moved to the aisle, stood firm and began again.

'We're going to do this in a more interactive way. This is acoustic not electric. Will you help me out?'

This time, a surprisingly raucous comeback. Now they were paying attention. In the back of my mind, I noted that this was like call and response in blues or gospel music. The subject was 'Applied Innovation', and I had a lot of pictures and models somewhere on the conference team's hard drive. To put over the concepts I had to *simplify, use my body a lot, roam up and down the central aisle, get closer to the audience and tell more stories*. In fact, all the essential ingredients of a great presentation!

I enlisted support from the audience. There's one four-box model about mindset I sometimes use, with Attitude on one axis (negative to positive) and Energy on the other (low to high). You can label the quadrants as the Walking Dead (low on energy and not very positive) through to Spectators, Cynics and Players.

That took a few lines of text to explain, when one picture would have done it. So I got volunteers from the group to *become* the visual and to play the different characters in the model. In the end, everyone in the room moved to a position that captured their attitude to the company's new and untested 'Go to Market' strategy – from Walking Dead to Players.

I was busking, but the sheer physicality of the exercise meant that people were alive and engaged. More profoundly, the senior team really 'got' the idea that too many people in the business were still 'spectating', waiting to see if the strategy worked, or were in the Cynics' box. When I described Cynics as people who *believe* they are only healthy sceptics, while they depress the hell out of everyone around them, several people moved out of that area. It started a discussion that went on into the evening.

Continuing the musical metaphor, I took the Greatest Hits from my talk and wove the session around them. Not everything worked out, but from the audience's warm response, there were clearly more hits than misses. And I finished on time, something I'd have been struggling to do with a full PowerPoint deck.

The compère was now back on form. 'Nigel, thank you. That rocked!' I don't know whether I'd really set the tone for that comment, but it went deeper than a nice accolade. I realised that because I'd been unplugged, I really had to rock up the material more; to rely more on expression, passion and energy – the essence of any good talk.

A business leader I know habitually presented to her people using state-of-the-art technology and multimedia. Often they were impressed, but not touched. I proposed to her the idea of going unplugged. With some trepidation, she developed the practice of presenting without notes, without PowerPoint, and spontaneously, without a lot of preparation. She talked more from the heart, drew on a flipchart and encouraged their involvement.

This was a terrifying experience for her the first time. She felt that without her technical aids, she'd had an arm amputated! However, the engagement and response she got in these new meetings was almost magically different from ones she had run with her former, at-a-distance style. She felt a softening of the boundaries between her and the other people at the meeting. While she continued to lead the conversation strongly, it was a conversation rather than a lecture.

'Unplugged' can be a great approach to a pitch, partly because of its freshness and intimacy, also because it can help you stand out from standard, technology-driven presentations. Think acoustic, not electric.

## *Sound and Vision: Things to think and do*

⏮ Listen to a talk of yours that's been recorded – even on a mobile phone. As a listener, what do you think of your:

- Volume
- Tempo (speed)
- Clarity
- Tone?

⏸ How visual are your visuals – and how many slides do you have?

▶ Get rid of bullet points, substitute visuals and HALVE the number of slides you have ...

⏮ Think back to where you've seen props used well.

▶ Find and use a prop that's relevant to your topic.

⏭ Imagine how you can remove any technical barriers between you and your audience. What would it feel like, to you and to them?

▶ Plan how to give your talk or pitch 'unplugged', and become more intimate with your audience.

## Sound and Vision: Your notes

# FIVE

# PERFORM

- ◆ Warm Up: Make Your Entrance
- ◆ Be Present
- ◆ The Body Language Thing: Elvis or Bing Crosby?
- ◆ Perform with Passion
- ◆ Use Your Imperfections

How you deliver your material is almost as important as what you have to say. This is true whether you are presenting to business leaders or schoolchildren. So far, we've been focusing more on livening up your content – now let's explore what we can learn from music about the art of performance.

There's always a strong element of performance in putting over your ideas – whether you're on a webcast, speaking over the telephone or in a lecture hall. In all cases you need to know how to use your body, face and eyes for maximum impact. Above all, to show your passion and enthusiasm for the subject. That's what will touch and win over your audience, getting under the radar of their rational or cynical minds.

Establishing presence with the group is important; your own depth of focus and intensity will draw them into the moment. We'll explore some of the stagecraft involved in this, find practical ways to show your passion and finish on how you can use your imperfections.

It's show time . . .

◆

## Warm Up: Make Your Entrance

A tennis player or footballer doesn't start a game without warming up, grooming their mind and body into a state of readiness. Musicians have their own warm-up routines. On his recent, unexpected world-beating tours (not bad for a then seventy-seven-year-old), Leonard Cohen warmed up off-stage with his band and backing singers by leading them in a Latin song, 'Pauper sum ego, nihil habeo'* – 'I am poor, I have nothing.' They all then walked onto stage singing, as a ritual for focusing.

Madonna and her team say a prayer together and hug.

All a bit over the top if you're just delivering a talk at the local rotary meeting? Yes, but it certainly helps to have a ritual or routine to get you off on the right foot. I'm often asked, 'Do you get nervous?' before a big presentation. The answer is rarely, but I do have my own preparation: a minute or two of meditation, specifically the best researched type, Transcendental Meditation. It's a simple, but subtle technique you do need to learn from a trained teacher, and totally unlike the kind of guided relaxation you might have experienced at the end of a yoga class, mindfulness or whatever else is currently available.

The scientific research (over five hundred published studies) shows, among many other benefits, that practising TM allows your mind and body to enter a measurably different state called 'restful alertness'. That's exactly how you need to be to relate to an audience: relaxed, but also focused. To be able to

---

* 'Leonard Cohen: Before the gig, a chant in Latin', *Independent* (5 Sept 2012).

hold the big picture while also attending to clarity of exposition, timing and detail.

I will meditate for just a few minutes, sitting quietly with my eyes closed.

When I open them everything looks a bit brighter, my mind is sharper, while my body's relaxed. A good challenge will bring the best out of you, while stress inhibits your performance.

Getting fit to present is important. Whenever I can do a good swim before speaking, I know I'm going to be more energised. Above all, you are presenting yourself to a group, and how you feel inside is more visible to the listener than you realise.

Whatever you choose, find a way of warming up and tuning in.

## Your entrance

When you're set to give your rocked-up talk, what kind of an entrance should you make – and does it matter?

James Brown, the self-styled 'hardest working man in show business', would have his backing band play a funky instrumental number while he peeped through the stage curtains, waiting until he felt the audience was sufficiently warmed up to be worthy of his presence. It could take ten or fifteen minutes, and would ensure he was greeted by rapturous applause. If only out of relief!

Microsoft boss and co-founder Steve Ballmer did his own James Brown entrance a few years ago at a big company pow-wow. Gesturing frantically for the audience to up their thunderous clapping and whoops, he hopped and bounced across the stage for two minutes, yelling 'I love this company!' It's a memorable start, but unfortunately for Ballmer, he was in poor physical shape, sweating and breathless after this fairly light exercise. But you have to say it was a memorable, even brave, entrance. How many other introductions to company love fests have gone viral?

What you *say* at the outset also sets the mood. I was once asked by a CEO how he should open his conference. I suggested four things to cover, in his own words:

1. Why are we here? (Mind)

2. Why I personally believe it's important. (Emotion)

3. What I hope will be the result of this day (Future) and

4. Why now? (Present)

I've tweaked this advice over the years, but I always come back to some variation of these basic questions because they work. You are making not just a physical entrance, but an 'entrance' for the minds and emotions of the listener to tune in to.


## Be Present

To present, you have to be ... present. Obvious, perhaps, but you can sense when someone is doing it by rote and isn't fully *there*.

Pausing helps. There's a wonderful English phrase: 'collecting yourself'. I see this as being like the moments when the tide recedes on a steep beach: the water is collecting itself in the silence between waves, preparing for the next onslaught.

Pausing and looking around the room for a few seconds before starting has a similar effect. The silence is gathering strength, and when you speak, it's as if your words have more power.

A Greek professor of engineering I knew – a world authority in his field – was particularly good at this kind of start. He would walk to the front of the stage and stand perfectly still, making eye contact with a few members of the audience. The hubbub would settle, and suddenly all eyes were on him. They could see and feel his presence.

Like the famous shampoo instruction that made the manufacturer wealthy: repeat! At any time in your talk, if you think you've lost them or you're lost in your own narrative – which usually amounts to the same thing – simply pause, look up and around and re-establish your presence.

In this sense you are the conductor of the symphony. You create the pregnant rests before launching into a topic; you control the crescendos, the balance and tempo of the piece. Most audiences respond well to this provided you're good-humoured and not overbearing in the ways you give direction to the conversation. After all, that's what you should be going for: a chat with one person.

## Be here now

The art of grounding the audience into the state of *'being here now'* might sound whimsical, but the difference between a distracted audience and one that's really present can be felt, almost touched, in a room. When you want their attention, you have to bring them into the room. Now.

Ian Taylor is a fellow speaker and friend who was simply brilliant at doing this. He's possibly the most curious man I've ever known – about people, places, art, new technology and music. In his talks, he would spontaneously introduce, early on, some incident or insight he'd experienced that very morning: an exchange with the hotel manager, a line from today's newspapers or an observation about the history of the city or building he was in. Almost like magic, it sent the signal that this is a unique, shared moment, and somehow the group felt it, too.

For Ian, a comment from a delegate at coffee break would become the springboard for an extended conversation about his themes of teamwork, leadership or innovation. He had simply drawn the group into the present moment.

## Switch channels

To be more present yourself, you need to have two channels running in your brain. Channel One is focusing on a clear exposition of your theme, but Channel Two is broader: you are thinking about the audience's receptivity, if you're going to cut some part you're running out of time for, whether you need a change of pace or tone. Channel Two is monitoring the *how*, more than the *what*.

Singers think as well! Tracey Thorn is one half of the celebrated band, Everything but the Girl. She's a successful author, and now able to enjoy music from the side of the stage. (She used to suffer from stage fright.)

In a radio interview, Tracey said, 'There's a lot of thinking in singing.'

She describes how her mind would be racing ahead to think how she was going to approach that difficult passage in the song. Thinking ahead matters: it's maintaining the big picture while immersed in the details. What helps you to have this free mental capacity is that you've rehearsed the content and aren't trying to remember it as you go along. This comfort with your material helps you to have extra bandwidth to tune in to what matters – the audience's reception. As a listener, I want you to know your stuff inside out (Channel One), but I'm strongly affected by how you connect it all to me (Channel Two).

Keep thinking – are you really having a conversation that people in the room are getting, or are you pushing against a passive silence. Then think ahead to how you are going to simplify and clarify what comes next.

### Ray Davies's Idea

The Kinks are one of the UK's most enduring bands, and their leader, Ray Davies, has also made a career out of writing plays, musicals, and prose. In an interview I attended, he described how even when playing large arenas, the Kinks gave the impression that they were just playing for one person – you. I asked him how they achieved this. He told me about an early mentor who had taken him to the top of a hill in north London's Crouch End. Beneath he could see thousands of lights: his coach told him the trick was to sing to just one of them, and the others would feel included.

Famous business presenter Tom Peters demonstrates this superbly. He often walks to one table in a conference room, addressing a tirade at that group while maintaining strong eye contact with just one person, until he reaches his punch-line. Miraculously, the whole room feels as if they are being addressed individually (and simultaneously relaxed because he's not looking at *them*).

## Break the 'fourth wall'

One of the best ways to be present with the group is to break the invisible force field between you and them. In low-budget science fiction movies, the actor mimes this unseen screen, convincingly or not.

Similarly, in a speaking situation this barrier is there, separating you from the 'aliens' in the audience. Actors call this the fourth wall – the stage on three sides of them, and the invisible fourth wall between them and the crowd.

Break it, and break it early on. Simply walking into the audience, making some eye contact, or shaking hands with one person, works like magic. It's as if the room has collectively taken a large in-breath, let it out and relaxed. 'Ah, we're in this together' is the subliminal message you convey in this way.

Again, this means breaking that dumb piece of pop advice to never look at your own slides; share a laugh, a reflection or insight *with* them and they are no longer alien or other. I've done this with a thousand people in the room, and it works. I don't know exactly why, but it does. It feels more like pull, less like push.

---

### Professors Who Listen

Professor Gabriel de Luca is a distinguished neurologist at Oxford University's School of Medicine, and his lectures are well known for being interactive. He will sometimes walk out into the lecture room and sit down next to an audience member, sparking a conversation that is – and feels – intensely personal. The rest of the audience tunes in more strongly as a result.

---

## The eyes have it

How can you tell when someone you're talking with in a restaurant is not really there? It's in the eyes: an absent or unfocused look, like the one I'm sure I have when I'm trying to catch the background music, at the same time as hanging onto the thread of a conversation. More than anything, your eyes let people know you're fully present.

Be conscious of what you are doing with your eyes. Are you looking down, into the middle distance, or out of the window?

I sometimes wake up to the fact that I've been a little static, and have mainly been addressing one side of the room. Without moving the body, just shifting my vision to take in those people I've neglected, often those at the back of the room, makes a stronger connection.

Eye contact of up to five seconds – that's a long time to meet someone else's gaze – with individuals in the audience, as you make a point, seems to trigger the mirror neurons of the others around them. You remember they are not blobs, but faces and personalities. *They only know you know this if your eyes demonstrate that you are truly present.*

Colleague Alison Weller once arrived at an overseas venue to speak to an audience of sixty. When she got there, she was informed – only half an hour before her talk – of a clerical error. There were going to be *six hundred* in the lecture theatre!

Alison had never spoken to a group this size, but she had in the past spoken successfully to an audience of 150. Retiring to the bathroom (where she considered staying), she decided to break the problem down into manageable chunks in her mind, dividing the crowd into four groups of 150. When she spoke, she made sure that she covered the four areas of the room with eye contact and body movements. By being fully present with four groups of 150, she was present and effective with all six hundred.

## Scripts and notes

A script in your hand makes it harder to engage with an audience. Your relationship with the crowd is limited as your eyes drop to what you're holding. I accept that there are occasions when the exact words are necessary: legal statements, investor and press pronouncements or an address at a memorial are obvious examples.

Two things tend to happen when you're reading from a script. Your speech pattern is generally less animated, more formal, less conversational, and your ability to connect with people diminishes.

Learning it all by heart isn't what I'm suggesting – rather that you have some visual or keyword summary, sitting on a table or even a podium, which you can move to and glance at occasionally. When you lose your way in a talk, you can say honestly that you want to make sure you haven't forgotten something, then read it. Strolling over to glance at your keyword prompts will normally do the trick. That's why any summary you make should be **BIG** and **VISUAL**. 'I'm sorry, I can't read my own notes' tests a group's patience, even in a classroom.

The advantage school teachers have is that speaking is usually only necessary in short bursts (unless it's the high school graduation day) before getting pupils to *do* something – on their computer or in their textbook. But even in short talks addressing their students, it will have more impact if said, not read. Your notes, if any, are like a map or set of triggers. An aide-memoire, not the memoire itself.

## The Body Language Thing: Elvis or Bing Crosby?

People hear your words and are simultaneously affected by what you do with your body to reinforce or detract from your points. In the same vein of giving you simple 'punk' advice, here are the three 'chords' of body language, characterised as three different people.

**Static Sally**. Stays in one place, at worst, behind a table or podium. The body signals this allows for are more restricted – hands can wave, yes, but the overall impression is one of reading a script rather than responding to the audience. Fine for press releases, presidential dictates and for a short burst, but it limits physical expression, passion and energy.

**Roger the Rover**. Wanders hyperactively and continually in front of the classroom or across the stage. This can be distracting as the audience is witnessing a lot of movement without it necessarily supporting the argument. Certainly it demonstrates energy, but it's often distracting. One 'Roger' I witnessed did this so much that people in the back row started betting on which way he was going to roam next!

**The Highwayman.** This combines the positive aspects of Static Sally and Roger the Rover without their downside, adding an extra dimension of intensity.

'Stand and deliver' is the Highwayman's credo – in the movies, at least. It's great advice for the speaker.

Yes, do move energetically (thank you, Roger) to a fresh position, but then stand firmly in one place (a bit of Sally) – and deliver! The power of your point is emphasised by your feet being strongly earthed, and it's as if energy is conducted upwards from this solid base, flowing up through your body and into the room more powerfully as a result.

The Highwayman posture also allows you to focus on using your upper body, hands and face more expressively. You can learn this by a bit of over-acting. Try being Italian, even if your version is rather hammed up from watching too many Sophia Loren movies or pizza adverts. You can't do it without waving your arms around a great deal, and it's hard to move your hands energetically without livening up your face, especially your eyes and mouth.

## Elvis and energy

You might be thinking this is phoney as hell; one of the worst accusations a speaker can face is being somehow *inauthentic*. Then listen to Elvis Presley in his early years singing 'Heartbreak Hotel'. He was a young, handsome, happy-go-lucky boy with a first record contract in his hands. Heartbreak was far from his mind – that would come later. He was using his emotional intelligence and imagination.

No one says, 'It was good, but he didn't really mean it.' A little acting 'as if' goes a long way.

Erotic jiving is now so prevalent in music videos that it's hard to imagine the anger that greeted Presley's first TV performances as he shaked, rattled and rolled in ways no white man had done before. The young immediately responded to what he was doing – expressing his joy and enthusiasm. Far from being the sexual threat the oldies feared so much, Elvis was simply having the most fun of his young life.

Gospel and church was the inspiration for the gyrations of his lower body. Elvis nearly joined a gospel foursome in his small town community; these groups were the rock and roll stars of their day.

In interviews, Elvis seems bemused at the outrage he caused by moving his body so joyfully. He said that's what he'd have done in church, and even in front of his mother. It was only sexual if you thought it so.

When he appeared on the famous *Ed Sullivan* TV show, the cameramen were instructed to only film him *from the waist up*. More like the often sedentary Bing Crosby than the real Elvis.

Well, even today a lot of speakers appear to be on the *Ed Sullivan Show*. They might as well be 'talking heads'. While you don't need to jive like Elvis, you could consider using *your whole body* to reinforce your points. This is where physical flexibility is useful when you need to bend over, twist or turn to give more energy to your words, and naturally it helps to be able to do it Elvis-style rather than in a stiff and restricted way. Yoga helps. A stiff body often goes with a rigid mind.

When your body is animated, it's hard for your voice not to reflect this. Pacing the room on a phone call will encourage you to use your hands a lot when you want to really emphasise a point. On an audio-link you can't be seen, but the effect of moving your body will be felt. A little touch of Elvis will help you sound more lively.

## An animated conversation

Back to your exaggerated Italian impression. The idea is to go over the top as a way of stretching, without straining, your expressive nature: you don't want to be acting out a caricature. My experience is that most people, especially in northern Europe, find it hard to go far enough. So overdo it with your arms and face, then relax a bit and you will be about right. Your intuition will 'get it'.

Ronnie Wood of the Rolling Stones is speaking intuitively when he says, 'There's an unwritten rule throughout music. I don't know what it is, but I think I've got it.'

Similarly, be natural but animated with your body, and you've found that unwritten rule of naturalness. Remember the concept of speaking to a large group as if you are having a conversation with just one of them? Well, it's right, but there's one thing to add: it has to be an animated conversation. As Zola said, 'We are here to live our lives out loud.' It's a good summary of a speaker or teacher's life.

Everything you do with your voice and body has to emphasise and underline your material, as well as exciting people and creating visual memories.

At least once in every talk, I like to do something physical and unexpected. Talking about the ineffectiveness of most corporate 'brainstorming' sessions, I might go into the audience and lie down on the floor, feigning the torpor that descends on a group when the boss announces 'I want your ideas – let's brainstorm!'*

Alternatively, I might physically act out parts of a story. My acting skills are negligible, but if I'm rocking it up like an enthusiastic amateur, it's surprisingly attention-grabbing. Being yourself may not be enough: being your *animated* self usually works.

---

* I'm advocating a positive alternative: prototype thinking, where team members jump-start the creative process by coming along with a first take, or prototype solution, instead of brainstorming cold.

I'm not a fan of the pseudo-science of body language, or of learning hand gestures, techniques for physically mirroring an audience and so on. My experience is that unless the speaker has really worked intensely at adapting these methods to their own natural style, you can see the joins in their technique. Think of politicians and their mannered, freshly learned body signals. Chopping, pointing and waving their hands, all too often to mask the vague abstractions coming out of their mouths.

---

### Expression Is Passion

In music, expression beats choreography every time. Future Islands are a tremendous retro-soul band whose album *Singles* was rated by many as the best of 2014. The stocky lead singer, the splendidly named Samuel T. Herring, is no Adonis, but watch him perform their hit 'Seasons (Waitin' On You)' live on the *David Letterman Show* and you'll see how dance enthusiasm can trump skill!

Herring also has the ability to sing his words with a bemused expression on his face, as if he's thought of them for the first time. Maybe it's an act, but it's very convincing.

---

The most compelling speaker I've seen broke all the rules of body language. He would sit cross-legged and talk for hours at a stretch about consciousness, science and meditation. Without moving his body, he moved you. It was all in the hands and the voice; he used rich analogies and stories to revisit the same point from fresh angles. You always wanted more, mainly because there was an inner quality, a consciousness, that made you think 'he really knows this stuff'. And in a very natural way he was radiating it.

For those of us less enlightened, using your voice and body

energetically helps greatly. As long as it's natural, and by natural I mean effortless and without strain. Ronnie Wood was right: it's not easy to explain, but you feel when it's right.

## Perform with Passion

Just as the music at the best concerts connects with the audience's feelings, so the finest speakers and teachers reach you on the emotional plane. Not because they are so clever, rather because they've touched you with something of themselves and their passion for the subject.

However, 'passion' is a contender for one of today's most overworked words – I'd like to reclaim it and make it useful. I've heard a talk begin: 'I'm very passionate about integrated supply chain management.' I'm not doubting the passion. I want to *feel* and be *shown* it.

How do you discover your passion and show it to your audience? Find stories and examples that illustrate your theme. Amar Bose, an engineer and founder of the hugely successful Bose electronics business, describes his passion for exploring how things work, his curiosity leading him to put his finger in a plug and get a huge shock – at the age of five! His relentless search for new and better technology is embedded in this tiny vignette. How do things work? How could they work better? That became his professional quest.

Then there's the Toyota factory worker who, on his walk home, would carefully align the windscreen wipers of every parked Toyota so they were exactly parallel, as when they left the factory. An anecdote that's a neat way of summarising the Japanese attention to detail and pursuit of perfection, which enabled them to become world players, only a generation after the desolation of the war.

## Make it personal

Personal tales are even better. When I introduce how I got involved with writing and speaking about improving the customer's experience, I might recount how I bought a religious icon on a Greek island. I asked the priest in the monastery shop the price – he picked up the artefact, kissed it and blessed it. I was sold. Of all the trinkets I've bought on vacation, only the inexpensive Madonna and Child triptych still sits on my chest of drawers.

In contrast, two days later I was in my home town of Oxford buying a newspaper from a vendor's stand in Cornmarket Street, now McDonald's-land rather than a place for buying and selling one's harvest. I was fishing in my pocket for the money while reading the paper's headline. The vendor placed the whole of his substantial forearm over the print, and said, 'You can read the paper when you've paid for it.'

Welcome back to England, mate! These small instances made me think of a spectrum of customer experiences, at one end a blessing and at the other a curse, giving me the idea of how you could make an exchange feel more like a blessing, framed up companywide.

I can then go into a genuinely passionate riff about examples of regard and great *dis*regard for customers in the digital age, like the search for a phone number on a modem utility's website: increasingly well defended and hard to find. Numerous tricks are played to prevent you ever speaking to a human being and disrupting the provider's cost model – it drives me crazy!

---

### Passion Inside

'You can't shine if you don't burn' was the note left by eccentric singer Kevin Ayers when he passed away in 2013.

Sean O'Hagan, *The Guardian*, 20 February 2013

Of course, your own stories and examples are what's needed to reveal your passion, and if you've had a near-death experience or Damascene bolt of enlightenment, so much the better. To borrow from street slang – 'Keep it real.'

## Protest!

Next, become a protest singer. I'm not saying mouth 'Blowin' in the Wind' or 'I Don't Like Mondays' – two very different kinds of protest – but express deeply what you really believe needs changing, improving or even unlearning about your topic. It might not be huge social injustice like Martin Luther King was aiming at with his 'I Have a Dream' speech; it's whatever you fervently believe is misunderstood, unfair or overly rigid in your field. What you bang on about in a heated dinner conversation about the topic, what you love and what you hate. Here lies your real passion.

And if you're thinking of censoring your true feelings, take a leaf out of Billie Holiday's book.

The renowned blues chanteuse would insist that she sing 'Strange Fruit', a gripping and stark protest against the lynchings of African Americans in the Deep South; it's still hard to listen to all these years later, and it's definitely not background dinner party music. Sticking to her guns cost Holiday precious bookings when the organisers refused her permission to sing it. She was adamant – hear my protest, or you don't hear me at all.

It's an intense example, and you may not have such conviction on the topic of, say, Euro regulations in the investment and financial advisory business like MiFID II. However, you do have your own opinions, and while these shouldn't override or detract from your content by overplaying it, show your strong feelings and you will engage with people better. Especially when you have to take them through some heavy stuff.

'Protest' means challenging received wisdom, so why not do that by turning the accepted canons on their head? French mathematician René Descartes' famous line, 'Cogito ergo sum' (I think, therefore I am) can be usefully subverted by casting it as 'Sum ergo cogito'. In the light of recent findings in neuroscience and consciousness, this opens up a fruitful line of thought.

Don't forget that the 'pro' in protest means *for*: emphasise what you are for, not just what you're against. Billie Holiday was *for* being principled, and for creating a fairer world. Similarly, you need to be *for* a better way of tackling, say, poverty, a blame culture or crime and punishment. It may be good therapy for you to harp on about what's wrong – too much of this and you'll notice the energy being sucked out of the room. It's like listening to someone else's bad customer service story. You're nodding, but praying for a swift conclusion.

Be strong in your convictions, but also be positive (or at least constructive) if you don't want to lose them.

Scottish band The KLF protested in an amazing way in 1994. They went to the island of Jura and burned one million pounds in banknotes, most of the money they'd made. I imagine they've needed the cash flow since, although they claim still to be proud they made this gesture as a statement about … Well, it's not clear exactly what. Apparently it's been hard to explain to the kids.

## Intimate thoughts

Rick Rubin is possibly the most sought-after musical producer in the USA. He's brought a depth and intensity to the recordings of artists as diverse as the Red Hot Chili Peppers, Slayer, Sheryl Crow, U2, Ed Sheeran and, most memorably, Johnny Cash.

The ageing star was out of a record contract when he agreed to work with Rubin. Passionate songs like the cover of 'Hurt' came out of this collaboration. The great troubadour was intro-duced to material he'd never have found on his own: 'Hurt' is a song about heroin addiction by on-the-edge rockers Nine Inch Nails. Produced by Rubin, it became Cash's epitaph.

To help Cash rediscover the music that was dear to him and full of passion, Rubin did a very smart thing. He asked Johnny to think about the songs he played for his family, sang in the shower, shared with close friends on car rides. He encouraged Johnny to play these tunes – some for recording, but all to help rekindle his passion for the things he held most dear.

When I'm coaching speakers, I ask them to think of stories or situations that are very important to them in their lives – transformational moments, ideas that inspired them, great highs or moments of countering adversity and loss in creative ways.

You can't demonstrate your passion without showing more of the inner you – your hopes, insights and experiences. Even your doubts, if you go into a minor key from time to time. It's your personality – from the Latin *per-sonare*, literally 'what sounds through' you.

What sounds through you the most? Hopefully, it's your passion and love for the subject, and you can't play-act that. At the risk of being vulnerable, you have to show why you are such an enthusiast.

Symbolic acts can convey your passion for change more than words. I was working for a manufacturing company where the managers were being driven crazy by a deluge of red tape and bureaucracy (more crazy, that is, than normal). As a way of saying, 'I hear you', the new chief executive went on stage and burned the company rule book – plenty of dramatic flames in a fire bucket – in front of his managers. 'Now, every-body – do I have your attention?' People at the top can protest, too. Why should the rebels have all the fun?

Don't get the idea that being personal has to be earnest and serious. It can be joyful, too. It's wonderful to see the video of the soulful Was (Not Was) playing 'Crazy Water'.* They are so relaxed, so into it, that it's contagious and extremely hard to resist moving or dancing to. Bottle some of that spirit.

## Be an enthusiast

Enthusiasm comes from the Greek, *en-thous*, meaning 'person inspired by a god'. There is something spiritual about real enthusiasm that can touch even the most cynical listener.

So bring your enthusiasm for your theme right out into the open. There are people who are enthusiasts about seemingly mundane topics, whether it's broadband speeds, EU legislation or companion planting in gardens. Make sure to seek out the enthusiasts in your own field, whether face to face or in their writing or broadcasting.

All day long we are faced with the choice to tune in to enthusiastic souls – however naïve – or to toxic people, the cynics or naysayers. While believing they are only healthy sceptics or 'realists', they depress the hell out of everyone around them! Science has been described as 'organised scepticism', and you can see the value and rigour of that. But everyday scepticism easily shades into the hollowness of cynicism.

While it's sometimes useful to anticipate the 'yes, buts' your audience may be thinking, especially in a pitch situation, don't be too focused on this or you can be drawn into a swamp of negativity. In life you are either a creator or a critic, and it's clear which one to choose as a speaker or teacher if you want to inspire and stretch the minds of others.

When we are asked about the subjects we liked most at school, it's usually the teachers we remember. We remember their passion and care. Above all, you remember the ones that you felt were speaking just to you, making the subject exciting and meaningful, often for the first time. They were

---

* It's on their 2008 album, *Boo!*

the enthusiasts, courageous enough to wear their love on their sleeves.

I remember hating physics, until Mr Hargreaves, a young, enthusiastic teacher, gave us a riveting hour on how the subject had excited him as a child, why he was following the latest moon launches, and so on. It sparked a lifelong interest for me – I'm sure you've had a similar experience. Think back to that person, that time. How can you inject just a little of that enthusiasm into your own lecture?

Kahlil Gibran* describes work as 'love made visible'. Allow the love you have for your subject to shine through and you will experience just how contagious enthusiasm can be.

## Use Your Imperfections

The professional in us would like to make our talk perfect. Despite what I've said about the value of rehearsing, leaving some room for improvisation and a little roughness around the edges is also likely to endear you to your audience.

Leonard Cohen provides our motto here in his song 'Anthem' (1992). He tells us to abandon the idea of perfection. He sings, 'there is a crack in everything' and strangely, that's how the light of understanding or inspiration gets in.

Allow your own light to shine through more clearly by celebrating your *im*perfections as a speaker. We are asymmetrical beings – one arm, eye or ear is usually stronger than the other. Similarly, we all have strengths and weaknesses as the transmitter of ideas or knowledge. In music, Guy Garvey of British band Elbow, Lucinda Williams and Neil Young have very imperfect voices and a fairly fixed range of expression. Within and through this narrow spectrum they convey great intensity and emotion.

Technically more gifted singers – for me, Norah Jones or Mariah Carey – don't touch their audiences (or at least me) with

* Kahlil Gibran, *The Prophet* (2013).

the same depth as a torch singer like the reinvented Marianne Faithfull, who speaks as much as sings her lyrics, and covers Brecht and Weill as much as pop. Classically trained opera singers often murder a popular song, forgetting the simple lodestone of melody.

You don't have to put on an act of perfection – after all, it would be an act. You only have to be at ease with yourself, your material and your audience. A great deal of this book is written to help you accomplish exactly this.

## On being yourself

The old counsel to 'be yourself' is still the best wisdom. I've worked with a speaker who crossed his legs, put his hands in his pockets and fidgeted with his glasses. Nevertheless, he mesmerised the listeners with a profound love of his subject: his passion for shipbuilding.

This is preferable to the over-rehearsed politician or CEO who chops the air or pounds the table to emphasise his or her points. It looks – and feels – too practised and insincere. *A committed amateur beats a cool professional every time*. So if your imperfection is that you don't project your voice well, do whatever it takes to make the setting and your tone conversational. In a professional arena with a large audience the technology still allows you to speak softly and be heard.

Perhaps you're not happy pacing the stage? Then create the conditions for feeling more relaxed. Preferably not clinging to a podium for dear life, but on a stool, or even in the centre of the audience, if 'theatre in the round' can be arranged. Then there's no chance they won't be focusing on you; you don't need to be strutting your stuff.

Another imperfection might be a tendency to lose your drift in the stress of the moment. It happens to musicians, too. A few years ago I saw the English singer Beth Orton making a comeback at the Big Chill festival after some time out having a family. She couldn't remember the words of a couple of her songs, but thankfully a cadre of devoted fans helped her out. She was sensational.

The audience usually wants you to do well and will help you out *if* you know how to appeal to their better nature. Hence, a time-honoured piece of advice that normally works: when you've lost your way, pause, look at the audience and don't be afraid to say something like, 'I've completely forgotten what I was going to say next.' If you're feeling bolder, you can genuinely ask your listeners, 'What was I going to talk about next?'

It doesn't matter exactly what you say – it relaxes you and the crowd, and that's the secret to retrieving your flow. The answer simply pops up. Done without contrivance it can also make the audience direct more empathy your way – many will have experienced what you're going through.

Vulnerability was also part of Beth Orton's charm. You are vulnerable psychologically when you're standing in front of others with nothing but a few words and some images to command their attention. So it's fine to describe how you feel – nervous, excited or whatever – *if you can convey this in a self-deprecating manner.* Jokes about your own limitations or imperfections can help bring you closer, provided they are backed with an inner self-confidence that nonetheless you still have something relevant to say.

## Don't 'self-erase'

Don't be an apologist:

'This won't be as interesting as the last speaker.'
or
'I'm not really sure I get this myself!'

Here you've tipped the scale and become not so much self-effacing as *self-erasing*. Then you'll get the audience's pity, which is not the same thing as their empathy.

I remember once writing an introduction to a conference that downplayed the importance of my knowledge, and even of the session itself. It was, I now realise, an attempt to be liked at the outset. An American colleague from the Tom Peters Group I was working with read it and told me:

> ❝ Nigel, it looks like appeasement! ❞

This was not a good word for someone who'd been in the US military!

He was right; I'd tipped over the fulcrum of the self-effacing/self-erasing scale. Being liked is an *outcome* of giving a stimulating talk, not the means to it. You, like the audience, are not perfect – and you don't need to try.

---

### Avoid Being 'Self-Erasing'

Self-effacing means too much apologising. For your slides, for having had insufficient preparation time, for not being as good as the last speaker, and so on.

Still doing this ten minutes in? We don't want to know. I call this 'self-erasing': you barely exist.

Am I being cruel? Possibly, and we should all feel for the speaker and make allowances. But will we? Drop all the apologies, ums, ers, and too many of the self-deprecating put-downs. Unless they are funny and relevant.

---

## Riskiness

Remember the idea of Imposter Syndrome? The feeling that one day you might be unmasked as a fraud because you actually know much less than you appear to? Anyone with even a smidgeon of self-awareness has experienced this at some time. Just make sure it doesn't happen when you're presenting to a roomful of people. Oddly, it's more likely if you pretend to be perfect, either in your mastery of the content or your method of delivery.

Feeling very confident in how articulate you are? Then it's time to make a small mistake – repeat yourself, try for a more ambitious story you can't remember exactly, and then they know you're a human being and not a computerised drum machine.

### Callas Rocks!

The legendary opera singer Maria Callas made mistakes – because she 'seemed to value expression over loveliness'.

Wayne Koestenbaum, *The Queen's Throat* (1994)

Put your attention on making this talk better than the last one, focus on the unique experience you are now going to create, and you will pull the audience towards you. Mindless repetition of exactly what you've said before won't work; a dull note will be felt in the air. They are here only now, and if your attention is also grounded in trying to make this moment new – for yourself and the audience – you have a better chance of connecting. *Especially* if you are not perfect and make some mistakes.

Above all, it's attitude that matters more than technique. Bob Dylan once remarked that he played folk, but with a rock and roll *attitude*. Similarly, you can approach any topic, weighty or slight, with the attitude of rock: letting rip, challenging convention and stirring emotions. You will make more mistakes when you really go for it: that's how the light of bonding with your audience gets in.

## Perform: Things to think and do

◄◄ Remember speakers who you felt were really **present** in the room. How did they achieve this? What was it about them?

‖ How are you going to speak to **one individual** and draw in the rest of the audience?

▶ Make sure you break the 'fourth wall' – that invisible screen between you and the audience.

‖ Think about where and how you're going to move in the room.

▶ Get in touch with your inner Elvis. Be animated – practise alone where you can't be arrested!

◄◄ What do you want to **protest** about? And what are your **enthusiasms?** Remember anecdotes or stories that *show* your passion.

‖ Think how you are imperfect – or just not very good. Plan how to use this downside in a constructive way.

## Perform: Your notes

# SIX

# ROCK THE CROWD –

## Audience Engagement and Participation

◆ The Horror of Q and A

◆ Hallelujah! Do It Gospel Style

◆ Rocking Up Breakout Sessions

◆ Avoid 'Death by Panel'

Interactivity and audience involvement are expected these days. Here are two very different models of involvement I observed at a Canadian music festival. You may not know the artists, but you'll recognise the different styles of audience engagement.

Frank Turner is a politically active English troubadour whose passionate performances are famous for getting an audience to their feet. He hit the right note immediately, introducing his set in French – always a crowd-pleaser in Quebec. Later, he sang one of his well-known numbers in the same language. Frank plays acoustic guitar and sings, and from the start he was leaping onto speakers, joking with the crowd, encouraging them to clap, dance and sing along.

Near the end, he announced that he wanted everyone to join in, but charmingly enticed the crowd to rehearse their part two or three times until they got it right. Then he joked: 'Now when you all come in together, let's imagine we're invoking the sleeping spirit of music and we can slipstream it to rock and roll heaven!'

We did! I've often baulked at enforced interaction and dodgy sing-alongs, but everyone went for it, ridiculous though the words were for a middle-aged man to be bellowing out in a Canadian park: a chorus about the joys of not sitting still, not shutting up and never growing up!

Just for a moment, we believed it.

Contrast this with a performance later that evening by another band on the up, playing on a bigger stage. The lead singer spent a great deal of time saying what a dream it was to be there, he'd never in his wildest moments have imagined ... etc, etc.

Two or three numbers in, he asked the crowd to sing along, and for a few seconds dangled his mike vaguely in our direction before snatching it back and continuing with his 'how wonderful it is just to be here' riff.

You hardly heard the crowd's voice. In part because they were taken by surprise, and unimaginable as it was to the singer, not many of them seemed to know the words. But it was mainly because the artist didn't know how to manage real crowd involvement – or just wasn't interested.

| FRANK TURNER | BAND ON THE UP |
|---|---|
| Tuning in to the audience | In own head |
| Rehearsing interaction | Going through the motions |
| Believing | Not believing |
| Intimate | Distant |

**THE AUDIENCE INVOLVEMENT SPECTRUM**

These two very different approaches to audience participation are directly relevant to the art of the presentation. At one end of the spectrum are those who believe in, aren't afraid of, and know how to get the audience's voice in the room – the Frank Turner method. At the other end, there are those who ask, in effect, 'Any questions?' – but don't really want or get any.

This chapter will expand your repertoire of methods to get an audience involved and engaged. You could begin by thinking about a presentation you are working on, and where on the Audience Involvement spectrum you would score your style of delivery – as it stands, and as you would like it to be.

◆

## The Horror of Q and A

The words never to utter are, 'Any questions?' A deep silence often follows, sometimes with a Mexican stand-off between speaker and audience, each daring the other guy to speak first. I say 'never', but if you really don't want any questions, this is the question to use. It sounds like you're vaguely interested in listening, but really want to continue uninterrupted with your own spiel.

'Any questions?' is a close-ended question, often delivered with the subtext, 'probably not'. Imagine you are shopping and the seller asks, 'Can I help you?' The closed nature of the question triggers a natural reflex – a closed response. 'No, thank you, I'm just looking.'

It's much better to ask, '*What* can I help you with today?' Even though this is just at the semantic level, it opens up the possibility of an informative reply. In a presentation, it means asking, '*What* questions are there?' Of course, this will be merely sleight of hand if you don't allow enough time for a response. The Frank Turner approach means genuinely believing that interaction is a good and valuable thing, and that your talk is a shared experience.

I'm often asked if I'd like to include a Q and A at the end of one of my talks. My reply is usually a 'no'. Why? In part because I like it to be interactive all the way through, and also if you call a session Q and A you get a somewhat conditioned response: awkward silences, rambling statements thinly disguised as questions, and the questioner who asks the same old chestnut every time.

It's also because I believe in the musical structure we've already covered: clear and compelling opening bars of your presentation, and a strong climax. If I do take questions, I then leave the last ten minutes to give a strong finish to my talk, to leave the group energised or reflective. Finish on Q and A and the chances of a crescendo fade by the minute – you may find much of your good work undone if it becomes an energy-sapping session.

---

### The King of Heckles

Bono was on stage in Glasgow making a worthy appeal to end poverty in Africa. 'Every time I clap my hands, a child dies,' he announced.

'Well then – stop fucking doing it!' came the response from a heckler in the crowd.

Opinion is divided on the actual words used. In any event the best response to a smart heckle is often to laugh along. And *then* continue with your serious point.

---

## What questions?

Make sure you don't fall into the 'any questions' trap. I don't feel badly about repeating this as it's still a feature of the majority of events I attend. Ask open-endedly for questions: '*What* do you want to ask me?'

Then allow sufficient silence for them to gather their thoughts, or their confidence if you are their boss.

Next, why not be the one asking the questions? Such as:

> How will this impact our margins?
>
> What did Stalin do when he heard the news? What would YOU have done?
>
> What will enable us to escape the commodity trap?

Even if you do this, the audience may be reticent to speak. Unless you've bored the pants off them, you shouldn't take it as a sign they haven't been listening ...

You know your material, where you are going and how you hope to wrap up your argument. You are physically much more active than if you were sitting in your listener's place, so for you *time moves faster.*

## Closing the perception gap

Here's the perception gap ... In the audience, you are probably hearing the content for the first time. Whether consciously or not, your brain will be comparing and contrasting, judging and understanding, accepting or rejecting. Alternatively, you may be taking a lateral holiday in your mind as something said triggers a train of thought, or you suddenly remember a phone call you forgot to make.

Attention moves in and out. It's the yin and yang of any dialogue: we are not merely soaking up information, but reflecting and connecting it to what we already know – and whatever our mind is churning over.

Here's one simple but powerful solution to close this perception gap: get people to talk to their neighbour for a minute or two about what questions they have. Then they will have plenty because they've had time to reflect, and also because they will have gained courage from posing one they thought was dumb, only to find someone else was thinking the same thing.

As I write this at the back of a state-of-the-art conference room, a professional facilitator is ignoring this advice, trying to cajole the audience with phrases like, 'C'mon, you must have some questions.' An uneasy silence follows ...

Getting people to talk to others also gives more reflective personalities a chance to consider their questions. This is such a simple idea that it goes under the radar of speakers who are anxious that there's not much time – and a lot of material to cover. Winston Churchill's comment that he liked *learning* but hated being *taught* anything, chimes with most of us. Covering a topic is one thing; thinking more deeply about it and exploring the relevance and implications of an idea is quite another matter. That's learning.

To ensure questions, I might say, 'Now, I invite you to discuss with your neighbours what questions, comments and disagreements you have about what you've just heard.' After an initial pause, the room is soon buzzing. Your talk already feels less of a monologue, more of a dialogue. You are on a journey together.

Disagreement is at least interaction. As Mark Twain said, 'Give me a hostile audience any day.' It's certainly better than a passive one.

After two or three minutes you will have **lots** of questions. It's really that simple. In a subtle way, you will sense the energy changing in the room, especially if you break the invisible boundary between lecturer and listener by moving among the delegates. I've found that standing in the middle of a group or sitting down to take the questions creates an intimate conversational tone. It's difficult to generate this mood if you are several metres distant on stage. It's the Frank Turner method, and you can do this successfully with a thousand people in the room. I have.

## Types of questions

What about the famous Socratic questioning approach? The wise philosopher was renowned for his dedication to edu-care – 'leading out' learning – through clever questioning.

'I use the Socratic method with my students,' a distinguished professor once told me. As I'd recently been studying this, I couldn't resist being a smart arse: 'How do you combine the six types of questions in your classes?' I asked.

A certain amount of bluster followed: it was clear that what he meant was that he asked a lot of questions. Much cleverer to call it 'Socratic', though, isn't it? I let him off the hook – I admitted I couldn't have named the six types either. For the record they include clarifying, probing, checking assumptions and questioning the question.

When you're told the six types, I think it's not much more useful than being handed a guitar and told, 'Look, there are six strings here – now get on with it.' I'm sure that it was the brilliant way Socrates played with these questions that was his genius, not running through a formulaic list of question types.

All teachers are thoroughly trained in how to use Socratic methods, aren't they? Rarely, in my experience.

So let's start with a more basic approach, which I didn't think was necessary until I witnessed so many speakers not getting it: the difference between open and closed questions. We've already seen this with 'Any questions?' vs 'What questions?'

'Is this clear to everybody?' is a closed question, usually followed by a general murmur of assent. It's a leading, closed question. You have to be brave to say, 'No – it's as clear as mud.'

So try 'What is unclear? What do you disagree with?' – if you actually want a response.

Once you've mastered this – obvious, but I see it ignored every day – then you can go to more sophisticated prompts to your audience. I would be speaking nonsense if I said this was truly Socratic, but here are questions I've found useful:

- **Probing thought**. 'What would have happened if the experiment had *dis*proved Einstein's theory?'

- **Driving your narrative**. 'How did Castro respond to the assassination attempts?' (Then go on to tell them.)

- **Rhetorical**. 'What if we decided to do nothing about this?' (You're not going to – are you?!)

- **Anticipating their 'yes, buts'**. 'You're probably thinking that our organisation has had several unsuccessful shots at this culture transformation – another bloody culture day – so what's going to be different this time?'

## Thoughtful questions

Thoughtful use of questions can make it feel like more of a 'we' than an 'I, I, I' conversation. Even if you don't expect or really want their comments at this stage, good questions help you to frame your points in a way that hooks the listener into being more of an active participant in your argument. More learning, less teaching – and more sensitivity to what may be going through their minds. You are allowed to answer your own questions.

When you are taking questions, make sure that you answer the first one concisely. Ramble on for five minutes, and you have set the tone: my God, we'd better not ask any more or he'll go on for ever! It's become fashionable to say 'good question' even if you think it's mindlessly obvious or plain daft. The impulse behind this is good – valuing the interaction, and *pour encourager les autres*. One twist on this, though. Do value the *questioner* – 'Thanks for asking that and for kicking off the questions' – but you don't have to say the question is good if it's obviously not. Try getting someone else in the group to answer it, then you're not in the position of putting someone down, which is a sure-fire way of getting the group to turn on you.

The best questions are the ones that get people to *think*, as much as the ones that invite them to speak.

## *Hallelujah! Do It Gospel Style*

Above all, it's vital that you convey early on that this is a shared experience, not just you at a distance giving out wisdom. Within the first two or three minutes, if it's a big auditorium, I often get the audience to briefly do something physical with their neighbour. Take each other's pulse, touch (very popular with the British) or whatever. I go out and join in, breaking the fourth wall between speaker and audience, and sometimes the buzz and laughter is so loud that it's hard for the group to settle down.

Great! I might say how I love to lose control early on. The tone is set. I want their voices in the room.

Now this is mostly physical interaction – how can you involve them mentally and emotionally? Let's go to one of the past masters of passionate oratory, the Revd Martin Luther King.

## Call and response

Martin Luther King's famous 'I Have a Dream' speech has been more pored over than almost any human utterance. It's pure gospel, and its musicality is a big reason that the words have penetrated so deeply into the world's psyche.

Call and response is at the heart of much of the blues, gospel and even modern rock. The singer calls out a line, then the choir (or audience) sings a response, an echo.

In King's speech you hear these echoes, deep soulful 'yessses'. And whether the crowd calls it out loud or not, they are feeling, 'yes – hallelujah!'

Now, it might seem a long way from the emotional words of a fighter for social justice to the talk you are about to deliver, say on a new cloud infrastructure to your IT crowd. So let's make this practical . . .

You can set up a line like 'who is going to change things?' If you've made your argument well, the response in the room will be 'us'. Leave some silence for them to feel it: it's an inner reflection of your spoken 'call'.

Or you can do it out loud. Maybe you'll say, 'There's only one way to fix this – do you agree?' If you've laid the ground well, you may get back a chorus of agreement. It's a closed question, but sometimes these can work to speed your argument on. 'What do you think?' may not be what you want to hear at this stage, despite what I've said about the value of open questions.

Feeling bolder? Then *ask* for a response, even if you think the answer is going to be mixed. It doesn't matter: you've created the conditions for a groundswell of interaction where even the passive listeners can come alive.

Here's a call and response passage I use when explaining how we all form perceptions on very little information. I've asked the group to tell me my life history only ten minutes into my talk, merely based on first impressions: how old I am, my education and professional background, marital status, the kind of car I drive, and so on. The point is that in a world of big data, we still use small data to make decisions – and don't stop to check how our perceptions match with reality. People get most of the answers wrong! I bring this out through a version of call and response:

| | |
|---|---|
| Call: | 'Could you have known that about me a minute after I started speaking?' |
| Response: | 'Yes.' |
| Call: | 'Could I have done the same with you?' |
| Response: | 'Yes.' |
| Call: | 'So then you got all the answers right?' |
| Response: | 'Er . . . no.' |

Putting over an idea like this has a nice rhythm to it, even though in this example I'm slightly leading them on. Doing it too literally may make you sound like you're a preacher in a gospel church. Imagine your announcement that 'We are going to diversify into the medical devices market' being met by cries of 'Praise the Lord!' and 'Hallelujah!' Not quite what I mean, but you can get the audience more in tune with your thinking if you find some means of provoking a reply or echo to your words.

To get a strong emotional and intuitive sense of call and response, try listening to blues legend Son House's *a cappella* rendition of 'John the Revelator'.

Here's the call . . .

Who's that riding?

. . . and the response:

John the Revelator.

He's doing both himself, of course, and you can't help but join in, even if not out loud. You are pulled in; you can't help responding . . .

## Duets

A duet is a great means of creating the feel of call and response. So far, we've been considering one voice, yours. Why not make harmonies with another. Or counterpoint.

I – or rather we – have done sessions where a colleague plays devil's advocate from one side of the stage, coming up with all the objections the audience may be thinking, but are too polite to say. On one occasion, we planted someone in the crowd to pretend to be very angered with what was being said. Only after a few minutes did the audience cotton on, and in the meantime they'd heard many of their own gripes aired and responded to.

Would you prefer a more harmonious second voice? Then rehearse with someone who has a tone or timbre that contrasts pleasantly with your own. Naturally, male and female voices work well together. Am I suggesting you sing the talk? No, but you can use some of the same devices. Normally one voice comes in sooner, and the other either sings a response part (that's the call and response) or joins in on the chorus. The chorus in a talk is your main theme, returned to throughout.

Suppose you are the 'lead singer': then your partner can come in with questions, a restatement of your central point or an example of their own that supports your message. If you're going to do this, rehearse like hell: get it right and you'll knock their socks off. Too many missed cues and impatience will set in.

Musical duets give variety as well as depth and weight to a song; anything you can do with two voices to add variety, create a dialogue and shine light on the topic from a fresh angle deepens the impact. Naturally, I'm bursting with musical examples to share with you, but the ones I love best are extremely sad, late night listens.* To keep it upbeat, therefore, I can suggest a quick blast of 'Sisters Are Doing It for Themselves', with Annie Lennox and Aretha Franklin on fine and complementary form.

### Interactive? What about Instrumental?

The desire for audience *interaction* can become a hyperactive exercise – voting pads, apps, and fun and games are fine, but all about being *physically* active. It can distract from more profound thought.

The audience is most engaged by what's going on in ▶

---

\* 'Hard to Love a Man' by Magnolia Electric Company (2005), and 'What Were the Chances' by Damien Jurado (2006). It must have been a good era for beautiful sadness.

their own brains. I call this **inter-mental, or instrumental**. What gets this inner engagement going are examples that relate to them and provocative questions like: 'Why are we here?' and 'Would anyone notice if we didn't exist?' The debate is both between you and them, and between the neurons in their brains. Inter-mental, or instrumental.

## Rocking Up Breakout Sessions

Active not passive is a hallmark of our times. Like this, snap that, tweet tweet. The expectation of an audience is increasingly that they don't just sit there, but do something.

If you haven't been party to a twenty-first-century style corporate shindig, your mind will be boggled when you see what people are asked to do in the name of 'interaction'. Dressing up, making movies, forming instant rock bands, painting schools, panel shows, competitive igloo building.* And that's just the conservative end of the spectrum.†

Perhaps it's a necessary reaction to the days of chalk and talk – PowerPoint being an updated version of the blackboard – and natural in an age where playing video games trumps passive watching for so many.

I believe this trend will have an impact on the classroom as much as on the conference venue (and already is). The teacher or speaker's role is swiftly shifting from being a sage on the stage to a guide at the side. The learner's new assumptions are:

1.   I can easily access most of the world's information – and a lot of its knowledge, and

---

* I have to own up to running one team session this way.
† Want to explore how elaborate company events are these days? Then go to eubafestival.com and see the awards for the most creative ones. I've been asked to speak there. Help!

2.   I can do it with a small device in my pocket. Am doing it right now, in fact.

A speaker today is less expected to be a know-all – students can and do download the information for themselves. What is desired is the ability to turn this information into knowledge, wisdom and insight, a process that's accelerated by interaction. This needs as much planning as your talk does – it's the only part of conference design that can keep me awake at night. How do you get their voices in the room?

## Creative breakouts

Imagine you have three hundred attendees, broken into small groups. How do you manage the time and energy level? Teams work at different rates, and some may fudge the task and get on their smartphones early. Others may be asking why they're having this discussion in the first place. Most critically, how do you hear their voices? Unless you and they have the patience of a saint, you're not going to listen to multiple report-backs.

I suggest that you keep the group in the same room, ideally at round cabaret tables that create an atmosphere for intimate discussion (not more than seven at a table). If people disappear to a syndicate room, you can't keep track of them, and it's great to have a buzz in the same space.

Music concert audiences don't break into other rooms – except to visit the bar! This usually occurs when the artist announces: 'Now we'd like to play some songs from our new album.' Most likely, the crowd will flood back when they hear the first notes of a familiar number.

In professional presentations you don't want any moments like this: keep them in the room and monitor the noise level and progress by moving around and tuning in to how they are doing. The best facilitation style is usually: *eyes on, hands off*.

To really 'rock', breakouts should be:

- Relevant
- Meaningful
- Stretching
- Fun
- Heard and Seen

## Capturing their voices

You should be asking questions that you actually want a response to, even at the risk of your listeners querying or disagreeing with your views. What helps most of all is to plan a feedback mechanism that captures the thinking of the whole group. Here's one that works.

Pre-produce A1-sized table mats for groups to write or draw the results of their discussion on. This works well for large events and smaller training sessions. The questions on them should be focused, proactive and not as open-ended as 'what have we learned?'

To keep the group engaged, I suggest you design different ways of processing their thinking:

- **A scale** (quasi-numeric). For example: 'How ready are we to make this new therapy a blockbuster launch?' The answers might be calibrated like this:

| 1 | 5 | 10 |
|---|---|---|
| | |------------------|------------------| | |
| IN YOUR DREAMS | NEARLY THERE | BRING IT ON! |

Then leave space for 'Your reasons for this score.'

- **Quotations**. A lot of information can be encapsulated in quotes – what people in the team have said, what is being heard around the organisation on this topic, or what customers are saying. For instance:

- **Their ideas.** This might be a list format to capture their proposals. No more than seven spaces should do it; the human brain can cope with information in chunks of approximately seven items. Think telephone numbers.
- **Space.** Finally, you might think all this is limiting their responses, so leave a space for burning questions or passionate opinions.

Then what do you do with the output? If it's a group of fewer than thirty, each team can take turns to present from their workmats. It's so much better than scrappy flipchart feedback.

For a bigger event, simply link a camera on a stand to the main conference projector, and immediately you have a professional summary of the workmats beamed to the whole group.*

---

* Thanks to the ever-creative Robert Maguire for this idea.

To break that force field between the teacher and the taught, bring one or more members of the team to the front of the room and become an audience member yourself as they speak. Switching the axis of power like this is a great way for the group to have the feeling that they are running the session.

---

### Get Them on Stage!

I once saw trip-hop artist Tricky bring twenty-five concert-goers on stage during his second number. To the horror of the security team, we danced and sang along with the band. The tone of the rest of the performance was set: everyone felt included.

In a classroom it means bringing a student up to the front of the room while you take their seat. It's amazing how this small shift of position affects the perception of power in the room.

---

Naturally, you and the audience don't want to hear more than a few of these talks, so you might encourage those with divergent views to come and present. You can capture everyone's thinking by creating an art gallery of these mats on display boards around the room.

You can also photograph the mats and email them to the delegates – along with a summary of the key points – after the event. The great thing then is that the conference has actually produced something tangible. Otherwise, it's all too easy for people to have a *black hole conversation* – interesting, but the ideas and exchange of opinions disappears into nothingness.

However you plan your breakouts, keep them lively, and short enough to stretch people, with a visual way of capturing people's views. A colleague who is a brilliant facilitator claims that playing great soul music in the background during these sessions keeps the energy up. It seems to work for him – and his audiences.

## *Avoid 'Death by Panel'*

At first glance, a panel seems to be a good way of getting the audience involved. However, they often fall flat – perhaps one panellist dominates, they're discussing a topic only two people in the group are interested in, and the energy leaks out of the room.

Physical distance can make it worse, especially in cultures where there's a tendency for the panel to be run on a high and far-off stage, like a military junta of old. This set-up doesn't encourage the audience to reach out to them, or vice versa. The trick is to make people feel more included in the conversation.

This is what I've found works. Applying the analogy of music, it can be useful to introduce each panellist like a band member: 'Here's Ruth Stern on bass, Luke Campbell on piano,' etc. You might have one slide that introduces each of them as you bring them up, one by one. At a high-energy event, even a few bars of music they have chosen can help to build up the atmosphere. Don't be clichéd – if I hear Pink Floyd's 'Money' being played once more to introduce a finance speaker, I'll have to leave the room.

Asking for questions from the floor too soon is not a good idea; better to have people able to contribute to an ongoing discussion than start cold. So if I am facilitating the panel, I might ask each panellist to say a few words about their angle, belief or particular expertise that might shed light on the topic. It does help to have clarified:

- Why the topic is so vital – 'why should I care?'
- What the debate is about – definitions and personal passions
- Dilemmas, challenges and paradoxes concerning the theme

Clarifying these three points at the outset should allow you to move more effortlessly into the first questions. Don't woodenly go along the row of panellists asking each for a kick-off statement – let it flow more like a natural discussion, where one individual can respond and build on the comments of another. Draw out some strongly held beliefs from the panellists and you've set the tone to bring in the bigger group.

## Make it a conversation

You might need to allow a discussion between delegates to get their best questions before hearing them. You can also prepare – you may have the luxury of asking for questions to be emailed, texted or 'apped' beforehand, in which case you have the advantage of being able to group them in subject areas.

In fact, 'grouping' is a good technique when you are eliciting questions live. 'That's a great question. Before we hear a response, who has another that's related?' This allows for more than the single interrogator to be answered, and is also pressing the 'me, too' button in people's brains. A different formulation of essentially the same question may provoke a more useful line of discussion.

You could try putting the panel 'in the round' on bar stools, rather than chairs, to keep the conversation relaxed and informal. Naturally you want to ensure that no panellist dominates. The parallel in music is an over-extended solo. Cynics believe that the CD format was developed just to make it easier to skip fifteen-minute drum solos! I'm thinking of the track 'Toad' by Ginger Baker of Cream: other drummers may love it, but most listeners feel life's too short.

So I have this word 'Toad' in my head* when I'm facilitating

---

* Not when I'm looking at the panel!

a panel, and know there's a time to intervene to make sure everyone's part in the 'band' is heard. The airtime doesn't need to be rigidly divided, but it should all flow as a natural, engaged conversation does.

Q. How long should panel sessions be?

A. Shorter than they usually are.

If you finish early, few people are going to complain, 'It was a great event, but we could have had a longer panel session.' I like to bring it to a small climax, asking each of the panellists to say in one sentence – or more extremely, in one word – what is the most important message they'd like to leave the audience with.

The musical structure of a strong theme at the start and a clear finale works well.

Think of yourself as a conductor – someone who brings together all parts of the performance – when you are planning and enabling audience involvement. They will participate well only if you send them a signal early on. *What* questions, not *any* questions. You have to be prepared to let go a little, take some risks and genuinely be prepared to hear difficult and even contrary inputs.

Listen for whether a silence is pregnant or a sign of leaking energy. Then vary the balance between your voice and that of the crowd; playing *with* rather than *at* your audience.

Finally, why not enjoy the YouTube video of Frank Turner's anthem, 'I Still Believe', a love song to his record collection. It gives you the feel of what it's like to get people on their feet and dancing: Turner's live performances are sheer joy. Take a little of this inspiration in planning your next talk or event, and you will be rocking.

## Rock the Crowd: Things to think and do

◄◄ Where are you usually on the audience involvement spectrum?

❚❚ Think how to (a) encourage questions from the group, (b) use questions in your talk that will involve them mentally.

❚❚ Think in terms of call and response – what's your 'call', and what kind of 'response' do you want from the group?

▶ Plan a duet with another speaker or audience member.

▶ Design team materials – as in the workmat format – which encourage a meaningful conversation about your theme.

▶ Work out ways of changing the axis of power: getting *their* voices into the room, bringing the students to the front and so on.

▶▶ Imagine what it would be like if your panel was a rocking band – excited, passionate and loud. Then think of how to create this energy.

*Rock the Crowd: Your notes*

# SEVEN

# ROCK YOUR PITCH UP – THE TOP TEN

- ◆ Get into Their Heads – Pitching to Bowie
- ◆ Make Them Care (Your Opening Bars)
- ◆ Think Beyond (Like Steve Jobs)
- ◆ Dress Up (or Down)
- ◆ Start a Conversation – Call and Response
- ◆ Keep It Real – Go Unplugged
- ◆ Demonstrate
- ◆ The Question Pitch – Getting Them to Write the Answer
- ◆ Fewer Words and Slides
- ◆ Less Time

The musical term 'pitch' is closely correlated with frequency, and in everyday language we talk about being on the same frequency or wavelength as another when we are making a good connection. This chapter offers you a range of creative ways to improve your chances of tuning in to the other party, and of being pitch perfect.

Pitching is the compressed form of presenting, where your purpose is to get a 'yes' to your idea. We all have to pitch, like it or not. Informally you might be proposing a holiday destination to your family, or suggesting new working practices to your superiors. You're trying to change an attitude, and possibly behaviour as well.

Then there's the more formal pitch across the boardroom table in front of a potential buyer, either solo or as part of a small team. Plenty of documents have been exchanged – now it's a vital moment to influence the acceptance of your idea.

A great pitch requires good presentation skills – you must be able to convey your theme concisely and energetically. Presenters pitch, pitchers present: many of the skills described so far can also be adapted to the art of pitching. However, the objectives of a lecture on the laws of thermodynamics and those of a sales pitch are quite distinct. You are usually pitching competitively, which means you need to stand out and be different. The provocations in this chapter will help you to do just that. Clearly you must have something compelling and interesting to say to the other party, or 'rocking it up' will be mere gimmickry. While it's good to show, you have to be able to 'tell' as well.

'Rock Your Pitch Up' uses rock here mainly in its street sense of shaking something up, making it more lively. I've had trouble controlling my indifference while listening to numerous pitches, so I think Kurt Cobain has it right when he rasps, 'Entertain us.' The listener will then be more receptive to the sheer brilliance of your thoughts. And they will certainly remember you: you've made them think and feel differently.

◆

## 1. Get into Their Heads – Pitching to Bowie

You may not have heard of Tony Visconti, but you'll certainly know him by his works – an in-demand Brooklyn boy who made his name by producing Bolan, Bowie and many other famous names in the 1970s. A competent musician himself, Visconti has a natural ear and the ability to knit together a composition that wasn't quite making the grade.

With this pedigree, you'd have thought he'd have been a shoo-in to work on Bowie's new record, eventually to be released as the acclaimed *Low* album. However, the past never counted for much in Bowie's chameleon mind, despite Visconti's successful track record of collaboration with him. A man bold enough to kill off his legendary alter ego, Ziggy Stardust, wasn't going to be moved by sentiment to stick with yesterday's winning formula.

So Visconti was effectively forced to pitch for the job he wanted so badly. The challenge with Bowie was always to bring something new to the table, and the producer's only card was a pitch-shifting device called a Harmoniser that altered the time-phasing of various instruments. Not a technology that would raise an eyebrow in our digital age, but certainly pioneering in the 1970s.

'So what does it actually *do?'* asked a sceptical Bowie. Visconti thought for a moment before delivering a line that is perhaps popular music's most brilliant pitch.

❝ It fucks with the fabric of time. ❞

You only have to look at images of the spaced-out Bowie of the time to know the genius of this line. The job was Visconti's, and he became a key contributor to the strange and acclaimed albums of Bowie's 'Berlin Trilogy'.*

The message is clear: innovators know how to get into other people's heads, to create an irresistible picture of why someone should buy into their compelling version of reality.

You have to have something different to offer, and need to be bold in stating it. Rarely do your best ideas come from cus-

* *Low, Heroes* and *Lodger.*

tomer research: creativity comes from anticipating what the receiver of the pitch doesn't even know they would like, but when they see or hear it, choosing becomes natural. What is really going to get into their heads? Be bold.

## 2. Make Them Care (Your Opening Bars)

I was speaking to one of the USA's leading brain researchers and inspiring educators on higher states of consciousness. He described to me how the brain's CEO is the neocortex, and when subjected to a new stimulus or idea, its first response can be characterised as simply:

> Do I care!?

Consciously or not, that's what the brains of those you are pitching to are thinking when you begin. If there's nothing immediately relevant or useful in what you are saying, they will switch off. The solution is relatively easy if you think about it: *make them care.* The survival instinct kicks in, as people do care about what they believe concerns, threatens or excites them. So don't use too much 'I' stuff early on; making the connection between what you are saying and what they are thinking is vital.

It sounds obvious, doesn't it? But the temptation to launch straight in with 'I' and 'me' material has been given in to by many a pitch team I've witnessed.

To be practical, I always make sure there's an image or key facts about the pitchee, their organisation, their competitive challenges, *on my first or second slide.* Rigid, maybe, but it makes me focus on them, not me.

An arresting opening statement also helps to hook minds that may otherwise go AWOL. It helps to make it:

- Short and memorable
- Focused on **them**
- Direct
- Relevant – ideally containing some benefits – why discuss? What is there in this for them?

Make them care, and do it as part of your opening bars.

Musician James Rhodes begins his shockingly honest autobiography, *Instrumental*, with the words: 'Classical music makes me hard.' He has my attention, and keeps it with his visceral, passionate writing.

Now I wouldn't advise you to use a phrase like this in the boardroom, though it does illustrate the power of a strong initial hook. The nerd in me is also drawn to thinking about whether there's a certain magic in *five* words: after all a great deal of popular music is built around the pentatonic scale. I'll leave that for the musicologists to ponder on: uncannily, it seems to work.

'It's later than you think' was the opening line of a pitch for consultancy business I once used. The phrase was relevant because we were addressing a significant competitive challenge to the client. I couldn't resist following it up with another five-worder: 'We need some healthy paranoia!'

Now without something solid to back this up, it would have been superficially deep – or deeply superficial. The serious stuff came next, but at least the potential client was hooked. This time we got the business in the face of fierce competition from household name consultancies who had droned on (we later discovered) about their global reach, competencies and – yawn! – case studies.

The only case study the client really cares about is their own.

'We can save you millions' was a commercially brutal opening we used for another business pitch. Again, it wasn't vapourware: we had some strong logic to back up the initial hook. The reserved Englishman in me shrank in embarrassment at such a crude reference to finance right off. We didn't get the business, but neither did anyone else, as the company disappeared up its own tail in a series of 'restructurings'. I'll save this line (if I can back it up) for another day when I can overcome the cringe factor! What I do know from a subsequent conversation was that the potential buyer was intrigued and interested in hearing us out.

### 3. Think Beyond (Like Steve Jobs)

Steve Jobs was renowned as a brilliant pitcher for Apple's new products – his ability to craft powerful one-liners to recruit key people was just as remarkable.

His pitch to hire John Sculley away from the comfort of his senior role at Pepsi was not accomplished by the promise of financial rewards – not a possibility at that stage of Apple's evolution. Instead, he hooked him with the tremendous line:

> ❝ Do you want to sell sugared water for the rest of your life? Or do you want to come with me and change the world? ❞

Jobs also hired top animator John Lasseter from Disney to his start-up media business, Pixar, by telling him that at Disney he could make great films, but with Pixar he could make history.

Not quite Visconti moments, but equally effective. The power of these lines is that they appealed to people's sense of doing something insanely great, of creating a legacy, of achieving more than the expected. It opened their eyes to new possibilities. Here we have the essential ingredients of a gripping pitch, and I propose that you spend some time crafting one-liners that will do just this for your audience.

In practice you may not deliver your one-liner, but the exercise itself is valuable as a way of sharpening your thinking, especially about the extra value you are offering and your ability to connect the specific task with higher and more exciting goals. Expand people's minds and show possibilities beyond their current horizons. Entice them into thinking 'why not?' and 'what if?' rather than 'yes, but'.

The notion of 'thinking beyond' can be applied to pitches that:

- Hook a listener in a sales situation,
- Appeal to your team's higher aspirations or
- Underscore your own value in a job interview.

In the last case you are pitching yourself. Go armed with a well-thought-out and even surprising statement – this should prevent you from using a cliché like, 'I want to make a difference.' Thinking beyond means beyond the obvious, the expected and the clichéd. You will stand out.

## 4. Dress Up (or Down)

Turning up to a pitch dressed as a beer can is obviously a high-risk strategy. But that's just what clinched the deal for an investment team who decked themselves out in the target company's product – with only twenty-four hours to prepare. Their bid won – the executives were bowled over by the audacity of the pitch, and by the rapid speed of implementation they'd witnessed. (For those not in business, 'implementation' is one of the new darling words.)

You need to give some thought to not appearing like a complete alien to the other side. Informal is the dress code of the day in more and more situations. I might wear a tie for a firm of lawyers or for bankers, but otherwise not. Donning an Armani suit for a meeting with retail buyers, mobile telephoning folk or nerds in the software industry can send the wrong signal.

But again, be true to yourself. There are few things worse than an overweight middle-aged man who looks like he's been poured into ill-fitting jeans and someone forgot to say 'when', as P. G. Wodehouse put it. Do you look like you'd rather be in a suit? Then wear one, perhaps one with some unusual detail, but a suit nonetheless. Red shoes are allowed.

A colleague put this well when he observed that you need to be on the cusp of their expectations. If you're too much like them, why do they need you. Too alien and they've stereotyped and judged you before you even begin your cherished spiel.

Isn't this all superficial when you really have something to say? Yes, but the human brain makes scores of millisecond judgements based on sound and sight (they're unlikely to be consciously smelling or tasting you), so particularly if you're a professional pitch team, spend a little time considering your look.

The value of considering your appearance in a pitch is that it also makes you think about the *tone* you want to create in a meeting. Is it authoritative and formal, or relaxed and conversational? The tone you intend to use should inform how you dress. Jackets at least for the former, open-necked shirts for the latter? You choose, but choose you should.

Former CEO of Apple, Jean-Louis Gassée, remarked, 'We don't need to wear our suits in our heads.'

'Suit' here is of course shorthand for stuffiness and rigidity. It's great advice for anyone giving a pitch – don't come over as distant and fixed in your thinking. Get closer – beyond the suit – and you have improved your chances of getting into the other's head. Even if you don't dress like a beer can.

## 5. Start a Conversation – Call and Response

When I think back to pitches that didn't go well, it's inevitably because I spoke too much. Using the musical analogy, there was too much 'call' and not enough airtime for 'response'. The catcher of your pitch believes you're not listening and are fixed in your views. Game over.

Kimberly Elsbach and Roderick Kramer are academics who spent five years researching the world of Hollywood screenwriters making pitches to studio executives. Working with fifty of these recipients of pitches, they analysed how often the pitcher was stereotyped in the first few minutes, sorted straight away into creative or not-creative.

Above all, they noticed that the most successful pitchers were those who could spark a conversation, which then became a collaboration. Put simply, if the catcher could be included as a co-creator of the idea, the chances of them accepting the pitch rose significantly. It became a joint solution, and most of us prefer ideas in which we feel some psychological stake or ownership.

So how do you start a conversation? *Not* by talking, I can assure you. The answer is to use silence and questions. All the more reason to make the talking part of your pitch short, concise and memorable, and to plan in potential moments that allow for a discussion to start.

You may need two or three break points in your narrative because you never know exactly when the other party will want to come in. You have to allow for the discussion, nonetheless. Silence is your friend, provided you've prompted the potential two-way flow of thought with an open-ended question. What do you think of the analysis so far? What more would you like me to say about this challenge? I'd love to hear your response.

The last one is technically a statement, not a question, but it achieves the same aim of triggering a conversation. Then – shut up! Don't make the mistake of rushing to fill the silence yourself.

When a discussion does follow, be careful not to skip too quickly back into pitcher/presenter mode. Probing and exploring questions help: what do you think we need to make this work? Tell us more about the threat from competitor Z? And so on.

Essentially it's call and response again. Doing this effectively means setting up the right lines (the call) that will invite a natural response from across the table. Unlike music, you can't predict the exact words of the response; like music, the listener becomes more emotionally engaged when they can join in.

*Instead of getting into their heads you are drawing them into yours.*

There's a fine line to tread here. The call and response conversation you start doesn't mean that you'll compromise the integrity of your essential proposal, or agree with every amendment or challenge they make. *Zelig* is an underrated film by Woody Allen, in which the main character has so little sense of self-identity that he morphs into being exactly like the person he's speaking to, in appearance as well as manner. Chameleon behaviour like this isn't respected: there are parodies in the film and TV industry of the pitcher who feels they are being rejected, ditches their own ideas and desperately tries to busk it with ideas they think *might* appeal.

Be true to your core – you'll be respected for that – but also be open to the other side of the conversation. In simple terms, you need to have a 'How do we make this work' conversation, not one that's just countering the other party's 'yes, buts'.

When you 'Yes, but' another's ideas too quickly, it's personal. They don't feel it's their *ideas* that are rejected, but *them*selves. Show some steel about what you *do* believe – you will demonstrate some passion and conviction this way – while at the same time giving an emotionally warm response to their contributions.

How you give your pitch is almost as important as what

you have to offer. Ensure that in the 'how' planning – you were going to do that, weren't you? – you actively build in natural departure points for a dialogue to start. The saying 'it takes two to tango' is self-evidently true, although in practice, this only works if one person clearly leads.

So plan how to *lead* a conversation, and you're tangoing. Allow them to engage with your proposal, and you've drawn them closer. Give space for your 'call' to be 'responded' to, and you've improved your chances of it being a hallelujah!

## 6. Keep It Real – Go Unplugged

We've already talked about this in Chapter 4: the approach comes into its own in a pitch situation. To go unplugged means to strip back whatever is non-essential. It can literally be the wires and the electricity that are unplugged, or in your creative life it means simplifying and allowing yourself enough time and space to get in touch with your inner source of ideas. In business it implies taking out all artifice and padding, focusing on the essentials.

The most obvious application of 'unplugged' thinking is to your performance and the environment in a meeting or pitch: without slides, videos or a computer. It's easier to express emotion when technology and a formal setting don't create a force field between you and others.

Apart from being low-tech, going unplugged is a mindset which implies an intimacy, an honesty of expression that means you are not trying to be too slick. You have to be prepared to say, 'I don't know', to share some of your ideas raw and unformed. Does this sound unprofessional? No, it's simply more human and open.

A friend was effectively pitching for the job of business school lecturer in front of a panel of worthy professors. His field was leadership, and so it was natural for one of the panel to ask him, 'How do you motivate people?' My friend sat back, paused and then said, 'I have absolutely no idea how you can motivate anyone.'

This surprised everyone, but a brief pause was followed by a spirited debate about the confusing and often contradictory state of the literature on human motivation, the balance between intrinsic and extrinsic drivers and so on.

Far from feeling he'd failed to answer the question, the sheer boldness of his answer impressed them. He got the job.

Using little or no technology can be a differentiator, especially if the recipients are hearing other competitive pitches, all of which have numbed them with slides or heavy research. Make it more of a conversation and you are halfway to selling your idea. But if you have to use slides, the 'four only' approach is almost unplugged:

1. **Covers the subject, your logo or your identity**

2. **Is about them** – a provocative question or striking insight that's relevant to *their* business

3. **Highlights problems**

4. **Provides solutions**

It's much easier to have a real dialogue when you're not worried about getting through your slides.

The message is clear: don't drown yourself in whatever technical 'reverb' interferes with the directness and simplicity of your thinking. Sit down with them rather than stand up. Do whatever you can to encourage a fireside acoustic session, rather than a distant, big stadium, electric performance. Move physically closer.

## 7. Demonstrate

The power of a physical demonstration came home to me when I was speaking at a series of product launches for a new generation of large format printers. A product launch is, of course, one of the few times you get to pitch to a large audience.

On stage behind me were the new machines with tarps over them. Like children with Christmas presents waiting in full sight to be unwrapped, the conference couldn't tolerate too much delayed gratification, so I was sharper and shorter. It's hard to compete with the physical: people wanted to come up, look, touch and press.*

So when you have a sexy new device or stunning piece of software, you have a natural advantage in a pitch situation: you can make the experience three-dimensional.

Senses, emotions and logic are three channels you can demonstrate through.

Senses first. In 1916 Edison, inventor of the phonograph, was having to pitch his machine to the American public, who were sceptical that he could accurately record sounds like music – and play them back. Columbus, Ohio, was the setting for him to demonstrate his device, and he did it dramatically. A famous opera singer, Marie Rappold, and a violinist played to a live audience, backed only by recorded sounds on the phonograph. It was hard for the listeners to tell which was the live sound and which came from the phonograph.

A big enough wow in itself, perhaps, but felt even more strongly when the sense of sight was used dramatically. Lack of sight, in fact. At times in the performance the lights were dimmed, and when they came on again the audience was stunned by not being able to guess if it was the recording or the live artists who had been playing. You can imagine a col-

---

* Not something that tends to happen to business speakers – which is one way we diverge from the life of a rock star.

lective 'aaahhhh' or gasp in the room. The singer also achieved this effect by stopping singing occasionally, allowing the phonograph to continue the music.

The public were sold, and even without the internet, the product went viral.

What I like about this story is that Edison's pitch used more than one sense, played with and confounded people's expectations and let them share an experience of amazement.

A tall order to achieve, I know, but if you build in even one of these factors you're improving your chances of having an Edison moment.

All well and good with something you can see, hear and experience. With a pitch for an intangible service, it's going to be harder to be so concrete. This is where emotions and logic come in. (Another meaning of demonstration is to 'logically prove' an argument.)

Demonstrate to your client that you are different and will always offer something more. You can show your essential difference by the thoughtful and probing questions you pose. Do a quick poll of what the client's customers think is *great* about them, and it's probably not what they're expecting. After all, the normal professional pitch is about identifying problems that need their help. Sales people even have a name for this: it's called 'hurt and rescue'.

Your 'something more' might be an offer to shadow some executives in the client company for a few days as a part of your pitch. Demonstrating your enthusiasm and passion for the job counts for a lot, and being able to ask questions the customer hasn't thought about helps to demonstrate your creative and logical thinking powers.

But don't try to win an argument with pure logic. I suspect your competitors are as clever as you – so you'll have to outsmart them by showing your passion and naïve enthusiasm.

The 'Amazon marketplace' we live in is pulling strongly in the opposite direction, driving us to make decisions on numbers and a click. It's 'contactless' as our credit cards describe it. Online auctions – a kind of lottery pitch – became fashionable a few years ago, but contrary to popular opinion, only around a fifth of winners of these auction pitches were decided purely on price. Rather it was a mechanism to *drive down* price.

You have to circumvent this distancing mechanism, to find direct ways of demonstrating your worth.

## 8. The Question Pitch – Getting Them to Write the Answer

The most literal way of using the questioning approach is to ask, before the formal pitch, what the answers should be. It's cheeky, but I'm often surprised how it helps both you and the other party to clarify thinking.

The golden rule is *never to respond to a written brief without questioning* – face to face or over the phone. Why? Simply because the written version is two-dimensional, open to wrong interpretation and assumptions. In Henry Adams's famous phrase, words are 'slippery things'.

Why not ask for a pre-meeting, requesting to gain deeper understanding of what's required so you can meet their aims more precisely. They can only say 'no', which is more likely if they've pre-decided that all the pitchers are more or less equal and it's a 'price only' discussion. In reality, it rarely is.

Failing that, ask for a video or conference call to pose your questions. What you're trying for here is to get more background, colour, emotion and a feel for what they think a winning pitch will look like. And for them to sense your passion for working with them.

On a call like this, you may pick up what they're really looking for beyond the written document. Use **probing** questions:

'What do you mean by . . . ?'

'Could you give us an example of . . . ?' and so on.

Make sure you use at least one 'rocker' or 'outlier' of a question, such as:

'What would happen if you did nothing?'

'What's your nightmare of a proposal for this business?'

'What is the single most important characteristic of a proposal that has a great chance of winning?'

It's asking them for the answers.

While there's a degree of risk here, the bigger risk is not to probe, finding yourself in a room where you've made a fatal assumption about what they're actually looking for – simply because you didn't ask. Often useful information gained by persistent questioning can help tip the balance in your favour when you eventually come to make your pitch.

At the meeting itself, you can use the question format to create a dialogue. Done right, it helps to make 'I and you' into more of a 'we'. Not all these questions require a spoken response. Here's an example of the kinds of questions I've seen used well:

| | | |
|---|---|---|
| **Scene Setting** | – | Why are we here? |
| | – | Why are we excited about this? |
| | – | What do we aim to provide you with? |
| **Other-focused** | – | What do we understand to be your real challenge/opportunity/problem here? |
| | – | Why do we think this approach may be right for you? |
| **Checking** | – | Is this what you want to hear about? |
| **Rocker/Left-field** | – | What's keeping your competitors |

| | | awake at night? |
|---|---|---|
| **Inviting** | – | What more would you like us to explain about our approach? |
| **Summarising** | – | In essence, what we're saying is X, Y, Z – does that make sense? |
| | – | What have we left out? |

Now if you're just asking questions, it can get annoying. Like the sage who was asked,

> ❝ Is it true that you always respond to a question with a question?"
> "Do I?" came the answer. ❞

Fine if you're a wise man, but not if the potential customer asks you, 'Do you think you can really deliver this?' and your reply is 'Do *you* think we can?'

Occasionally you can get away with this, but remember that in most pitch situations, it's assumed that you do the initial talking while they sit in the theatre box like the two grumpy old men in the *Muppets*, Statler and Waldorf, unkindly critiquing all that's going on below.

Nevertheless, you have to break this barrier between performer and critic, to pull them in by questioning. Unlike classroom situations, it's hard to *make* them engage. Don't use all the types of questions I've indicated above; if you have to choose, you can achieve a lot with scene-setting, checking and summarising. And make sure there are one or two 'rockers' in there. Ones I've used include:

Do you really think banking is boring?
Would anyone notice if your company didn't exist?
Would you like to hear why we think you're asking the
   wrong questions with this brief? (High risk!)

The TV detective Columbo learns by asking what are apparently the *dumbest* questions – they're not, they're simply the ones everyone has *assumed* they know the answer to, or simply aren't important. Frequently my customers say these 'dumb', direct, assumption-checking questions were the best ones.

One last thing – as Columbo would say. A question-based pitch is not a set of clever techniques, but a mindset. People will easily feel manipulated if they sense your line of questioning is leading them on. Having a questioning mindset means you are genuinely interested in them, their organisation, their aims, problems and difficulties. This means favouring the kind of questions that are direct, honest and, above all, make them think. When you can achieve this, they will also be thinking about *you*.

Suppose your mindset is that this is a rather boring potential deal with a rather boring customer? Then it's time to rock up your attitude: find an enthusiast, someone who really loves this industry, or the making of deals. Slipstream a bit of their passion, and this will show itself in your approach.

## 9. Fewer Words and Slides

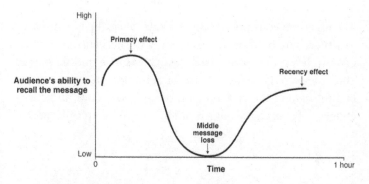

Cutting down on the number of points you are making can reduce the chances of 'middle message loss' between your opening and close. As audiences tend to remember the first and last parts of a talk due to the primacy and recency effects (see p. 19), to maximise their ability to recall the message later, you need more beginnings and ends, and fewer middles! Middle message loss can be made even worse by overwhelming everyone with dozens of very wordy slides.

## 10. Less Time

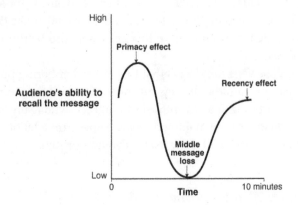

The less time your presentation or talk takes, the less message loss there will be. You can lose a lot of the audience's attention even in ten minutes, as visualised above. The middle part of your message is always at risk of being lost in favour of the beginning and the end, but you can improve your audience's chances of overall message recall by making your talk shorter.

# PART III

# Achieving mastery in speaking

# EIGHT

# GET EXPERIENCED – LEARNING FROM THE MASTERS

- ◆ Learn from the Masters
- ◆ Be an Apprentice
- ◆ Put in the Time (but Wisely!)
- ◆ Expand Your Mind

You're unlikely to become a great speaker overnight. Similarly, great musicians don't spring magically from the head of Zeus.

The learning and preparation you put in to master your craft may be a hundred times the amount of minutes you eventually speak or play for.

Because we can all speak, we assume that giving talks in public is just a small extension of this ability. It's not. Speaking to others is a craft we have to work at, and we can take great inspiration from the way musicians develop their skills. It's called 'paying your dues'. You've earned the right to succeed in four ways: following the masters, doing your apprenticeship, investing the time and smart practice.

Our companion on this journey is the legendary guitarist Jimi Hendrix. His brief, meteoric stardom in the late 1960s was heralded as something entirely original, an unforeseen bolt of musical genius that appeared from nowhere, only to disappear tragically with his untimely death in 1970. But Hendrix did his time and paid his dues to become the star we remember; we can learn a lot from his musical development, although I wouldn't advocate following him in his extra-curricular activities.

◆

## Learn from the Masters

At the heart of Hendrix's guitar pyrotechnics was the blues, and particularly the great exponents of blues, rock 'n' roll and R&B. Electric guitar great Albert Collins coached Jimi, and Hendrix travelled to visit the great master of urban electric blues, Muddy Waters.

Listen to Hendrix's 'Red House': it's a straight, twelve-bar blues, shot through with his uniquely expressive guitar lines. The audience would hush when Jimi started this number, the silence an unconscious appreciation for an older magic that was being invoked.

Even more strikingly, his 'Voodoo Chile' compresses into fifteen minutes the history of different blues styles as they emerged. Jimi had learned from the masters.

So who are the masters in your field, or those you regard as the most brilliant speakers and communicators? Who is your Muddy Waters? Today we have access to a universal library of speeches, video clips, sometimes whole lectures – whether it's Steve Jobs talking to university students in his famous Stanford Commencement speech in 2005 (surely the modern template for a motivational speech), TED talks, Martin Luther King, Malala Yousafzai or Winston Churchill. Research and draw inspiration from the greats in your field.

## Creative copying

A tip about observing: watch for *how* the speaker structures and emphasises their content, as much as for *what* they are saying. Copying can be creative. In his book *The Zen of Creativity*, writer John Daido Loori describes a class where a multi-cultural audience is asked simply to copy some calligraphy as accurately as they can. The Westerners, with a mindset that you have to be *different* to be original, produced their own 'interpretations' of the lettering. The Japanese produced very accurate copies.

The lesson is counterintuitive*: Students who practised the strokes repetitively developed greater confidence and skills, and without trying for it their own originality started to shine through.

The creative self emerges from being a faithful copier – and this applies to music and the art of speaking. The truth of Loori's description is that even if you attempt to copy precisely the style, body language and speech patterns of great orators, it will inevitably be refracted through the prism of your own personality. It will be different because *you* are different and unique.

Don't be reticent about observing and copying what great speakers do well, and also consider those who are the most challenging or controversial. The 'protest' singers of speaking, if you like. You will pick your own favourites, which is already a significant step in honing a style that feels true to yourself and your material, one that fits you.

## On originality

We aspire to 'originality', but the very concept can be divisive because it's usually understood to be a rare gift reserved for

* When people say 'counterintuitive', they often mean 'counter-*logical*', expressing an intuitive truth.

### Losing Passion? Visit the Circus

A few years ago, I visited Cirque du Soleil's HQ in Montreal. Here they make the costumes, audition and practise. It's on the site of an old wasteground bought from the City Council for $1.

Creative Director Lyn Heward told me the advice she gives to performers who have lost some of their passion. She gets them to go to new, fringe, exciting shows to rediscover what got them into their strange profession in the first place. It usually works!

Similarly, there's no substitute for watching the old masters and the radical new thinkers in your own field or profession: their passion can touch and rekindle your own.

the precious few. 'Origin' just means 'from the source', something from which all else is birthed.

One way to the source is to revisit the original thinkers and masters of speaking in your own field. Don't rush the idea of becoming more original yourself; our current love affair with the new and the different for its own sake is shallow. It helps to know what we are different *from*, and we know this best by learning from the masters, and not being afraid to copy shamelessly.

Watch great speakers online, while reflecting on *what* they do that makes them so riveting, amusing or convincing. Even better, attend live lectures by speakers you admire.

Obvious advice? Yes, but the obvious is often overlooked, especially because we mistakenly believe speaking publicly is not very different from speaking socially. It ain't so. Whether you want to be a professional speaker or just give a lesson a bit better, it's a craft to acquire through observation, and most of all, trying it out …

## Be an Apprentice

Hendrix played with many bandleaders such as Ike Turner, Curtis Knight and Little Richard. He lived the life of the itinerant guitar player, catching a bus to far-flung venues on the chitlin' circuit. Hendrix wasn't the best apprentice in the world, as he often missed the bus! He was fired from his first gig in the basement of a synagogue, Seattle's Temple De Hirsch, and also by Little Richard and Ike Turner.

However, he learned the hard way how to accompany others, stretch his own musical vocabulary and simply play in a band. Similarly, your own apprenticeship might be shadowing someone you regard as a great teacher or speaker. I've been lucky enough to do this with two of the world's great business presenters.

---

### Start as a Tribute Band

Authenticity is the goal to aim for, meaning your own, original material rather than being a 'covers' band. But most of the greats started by copying – the Rolling Stones' first aim was just to bring the music they loved, black r 'n' b, to a white audience. They started more or less as a tribute band to Muddy Waters.

---

Learning was by *experience* – observing, trying, failing, trying again, improving. A never-ending journey if you are serious about your craft.

Best-selling author Tony Buzan, inventor of mind maps and charismatic presenter, coached me relentlessly in my early days of business speaking. He taught me to use as many of the senses as possible in presenting, and on one memorable Italian business trip even improved my swimming and all-round fitness as preparation for speaking energetically.

Another mentor I followed closely was Tom Peters, author of the popular *In Search of Excellence,* and famed for the intensity and inspiration of his talks. While Tom didn't coach me directly, seeing him speak many times in different countries and settings was enough to dramatically accelerate my own learning. One of Tom's great gifts is taking as an example something small and specific that most people in the room have experienced – for instance, the illegibility of tiny text on hotel shampoo and moisturiser bottles. 'My God, the shit I've put on my head!' would be his punchline. He would then turn this humorous example into a rocking little number about the difficulty in life and business of understanding the perceptions of another.

Being an apprentice can take many different forms. Ideally, find a good coach. Face to face is best, but if not, there are also virtual learning modules online. And Skype can work for some people. Even if you are an experienced lecturer you will find something new and valuable if you are prepared, even briefly, to adopt the mindset of an apprentice.

## Observe and learn

Observation is another way to improve – it's what I did with Tom Peters – but it's *focused* observation that pays dividends. Watch for the 'how' more than the 'what'. Try this: *focus on everything yellow.*

A famous photographer was teaching a group of executives to be more creative. He gave them a strange-sounding assignment: go out with a camera and photograph *only yellow objects*. His point? By narrowing down our focus, we become more observant. Otherwise the canvas of possibilities is too broad. In observing other speakers, this means screening out a lot and focusing on a few variables, like:

- How did they open and close the talk?
- How did they establish presence?
- How did they use stories?
- Was there a clear logic?
- How did they deal with questions?

Mentally photograph just these yellow threads and you will have plenty to help you improve.

I never saw Hendrix live (though standing outside the hall he was playing in, I certainly *heard* him, as did most of my home town!). So here's the next best thing: I have learned a great deal from observing a guitarist in the same league, singer-songwriter Richard Thompson. He's been rated for years as one of the world's top players, especially by other guitarists.

## A modern master

Thompson was the guitarist in folk-rock pioneers Fairport Convention,* though don't stereotype him as an old folkie. Often he fronts an electric band playing blistering solos that Hendrix himself wouldn't have sniffed at. In fact as a precocious seventeen-year-old in London's thriving sixties music scene he did play with Jimi at all-nighters.

His other mode of playing is as a lone acoustic guitarist and singer, where his self-accompaniment is so skilled that it often sounds like two guitarists on stage.

Blues guitarist Bonnie Raitt, who has covered several Thompson numbers, said that when she first saw him play she wanted to leave the hall and break both her wrists because she knew that neither she, nor almost anyone, could play with that sustained level of skill and intensity.

* ... and a big part of why the band was signed by sixties musical pioneer Joe Boyd.

What I've learned, particularly from seeing Thompson play solo, is three things: *intensity, light and shade* and *timing*.

> ### Listen to the Bass
>
> One way to groove your ability to observe and listen effectively is to warm up with music. Try listening to just one instrument on a track – for instance, the bass in Cream's 'Badge' or in the Rolling Stones' 'Miss You' (surely their best dance number). Screen out the rest and you are listening differently and yet picking up the whole, seen from a new perspective.
>
> Related to your talk, the bass is of course the rhythm, the beat, and earthiness of what you are saying. What would it mean to have 'more bass' in your lecture?

The mechanism by which a presentation touches an audience is hard to define, but a certain intensity of conviction, even if softly spoken, is one of the essential components. When Thompson goes into a song, there is a short pause, almost a gathering up of psychic strength, before he pours himself into the number. I've never seen him play a song without giving it the full-on treatment, evoking the feelings that the song is played *through* him as much as by him.

If you've given presentations, you'll recognise the moment, often accompanied by a kind of dead silence, that you're losing (or have lost) an audience. Maybe you've been dwelling on one point too long, told one too many anecdotes or hit them with too many histograms. Whenever I sense this coming, at the corner of my mind is a Thompson performance – so I pause, take time to really look at the audience, and then plunge into a fresh topic with renewed intensity. It usually works. Watching him perform so often seems to have ingrained the tendency somewhere in my unconscious.

Then there's light and shade. Thompson is not known for chirpy ballads, to say the least. In fact, he's quite likely to introduce a number with a cheery line like, 'no evening is complete without a good murder ballad. And there's only twelve verses!' *Watching the Dark* is the apt title of a song compilation from his early days.

So where does the 'light' come from? In performance, he will throw in a humorous number he might have written for one of his kids, and he's also a witty and self-effacing raconteur. Not everyone likes this; for some it can break the spell the music has cast, but for me it's a lesson in balancing the light with the heavy, the humour with a serious point. When you can make people laugh, they are more open to looking more deeply into the idea that lies beneath the surface of thought. In other words, an *in*sight.

This is all to do with *tone*, musically or in a presentation. Get the tone right and your audience will follow.

Timing is the other intuitive lesson I've learned. Thompson never finishes a song until he finds the perfect ending. It may be a sudden chop or a delicate note, but it's always aimed at leaving you with a sense that *no other finish could have worked*. And it seems to be improvised to fit the moment, not necessarily the same as on the recorded version.

### Apprentice Yourself to Curiosity

Fresh-faced Robert Zimmerman arrived in New York's Greenwich Village music scene in 1961. He then set about watching, listening to or playing with anyone and everyone he heard was good, across many musical genres. Much of it found its way into his playing. Like him or not, nobody sounded like Dylan, and yet he started as a copier of all that was best in other people's sounds. Do great artists steal? Maybe. But copying is a good place to begin.

In the same way, the state of mind or emotion you leave an audience with is often what's remembered the most. I've found it helps to have two or three different possible endings to a presentation, and try to end on the one that resonates most with this specific group, on this unique day. Like Thompson, I'm not going to finish until I've found the right note.

Going to live talks (and music) is a great way to apprentice yourself to the art of speaking. You can also achieve some of this effect just by watching speakers online or on TV, noticing how a news story is structured or an eloquent debater makes their points. Note down what you observe – you probably won't remember later, especially the emotional effect. You're writing your own Apprentice's Journal of speaking skills, which may be as useful as anything I, or writers like me, can tell you.

## Put in the Time (but Wisely!)

You've probably heard about the 10,000 hours principle;* the time you need to invest to be at home with your field, to achieve mastery in it. It's the hours Jobs and Gates put into learning, experimenting and creating with the early computers, and roughly the time the Beatles played together in Hamburg, performing six to eight hours a day, for weeks on end.

The figures that capture it most succinctly are that a music *student* may only have to put in around 1,000 hours, a music *teacher* 3–4,000, while a music *professional* gets to 10,000 hours.

Hendrix would be in his apartment making breakfast with his guitar around his neck. Playing, experimenting, practising, even in bed. Perhaps someone should write a blues for the guitarist's girlfriend: a part of her must fear he'd rather make love to a few pounds of steel, wood and wire. As a professional speaker, I've sometimes woken up speaking out loud – often the bits that I could have done better, or forgot to say, or just rehearsing a new idea I've been working on. At least that's how I would explain it if I ever have to consult a psychiatrist.

* For a fuller exposition, read Malcolm Gladwell's *Outliers* (2008).

### Do a Picasso

I am always doing that which I cannot do, in order that I may learn how to do it.

## Deliberate practice

You have to use your time wisely. Repeating the same passage in the same way over and over would be like the old quip about someone having thirty years of experience – but it's only been one year, repeated thirty times.

The trick is to use 'deliberate practice'. Consciously working on what you're not good at, what needs improving, experimenting with a new theme or style of delivery. This is how your practice can pay huge creative dividends.

An extraordinary video describes the deliberate practice approach. It's called: *shorter clarissa three.mov,* featuring a study conducted by Australian music psychologists McPherson and Renwick. Over a fifteen-minute period a teenage girl, who has no idea how to play a piece of music on the clarinet, learns by intensively reworking the difficult passages. And what relearning! She becomes such an adept player in a few minutes that writer Daniel Coyle says the movie should be called[*]:

*THE GIRL WHO DID A MONTH'S WORTH OF PRACTICE IN SIX MINUTES*

She was hearing errors, fixing them, constantly trying to link the part to the whole, practising in a highly focused fashion to remove faults in her playing.

The speaker can take a leaf here from the music student's book. Musicians can *hear* what they are playing, which gives an immediate feedback loop to the brain to adjust the playing next time. The message is that we have to get our ideas out

[*] Daniel Coyle, *The Talent Code: Greatness Isn't Born It's Grown* (2009).

there, preferably hear them spoken out loud so we can test how clear we are in our thinking, how resonant in our delivery. To re-hearse is to re-hear – and to learn in the process.

Doubtless some geek with a wicked algorithm could track Hendrix's routine to see if his practice was deliberate or repetitive. I don't think it's necessary. His playing was always pushing out the boundaries of what was possible, and in the year before his untimely death he'd incorporated more jazz and experimental sounds into his guitar performances.

Specific things to deliberately practise – preferably out loud – are the energy and tone of your voice, your clarity of explanation and even the punchlines to your stories.

Brian Eno, the great pioneer of ambient music, talks about the power of *releasing* an idea, putting it out there to see how others respond. The word 'release' is appropriate for the artist, who has been hearing many conversations inside their own heads and needs to let it fly to see how it lands with an audience.

The surprising experience most people have is that it's harder to speak convincingly to those who know you well; they are probably more critical and less forgiving than a bigger audience. Survive this baptism by fire and your deliberate practice will bear fruit.


## Expand Your Mind

Here's a clue for your own development as a speaker: boredom can be creative! Jimi confessed in the latter part of his career that he was bored with the blues and its narrow palette of themes – my old woman/man trouble, alcoholism and poverty. This boredom fired him to extend his subject matter and the influences he introduced to his work.

Black musicians didn't like the fact that he would listen to all kinds of music, memorably covering and turbo-charging songs like the Troggs' 'Wild Thing' and Dylan's 'All Along the

Watchtower'.* For Jimi, there was almost no subject matter that couldn't be included, especially his own personal philosophy, science fiction and explorations in 'inner space'. We have to remember that he was in his prime at the height of space missions, and what a great source of inspiration this was for many. His boredom and restlessness with his roots propelled him to pioneer totally new ways of playing. His poignant, fragmented rendition of 'The Star-Spangled Banner' is hard to take in the first time round: he was extending the guitar's repertoire of expressive possibilities.

### On Practice

Practice isn't the thing you do once you're good. It's the thing you do that makes you good.

Malcolm Gladwell

Similarly, if you have been speaking regularly, there are probably bits of your talk that you are bored with. Stories you've told too often, examples that need replacing, fresh research you could be introducing. One way to keep your audience alive is to continually shake yourself up, pushing yourself into experimental avenues of thought.

## Find new sources of inspiration

To expand your mind also means to draw on different influences and genres of thought beyond the obvious. Just as Hendrix shook up the somewhat repetitive structures of traditional blues and integrated fresh sounds, you need to explore parallel fields that add richness and depth to your own thinking.

Darwin moved between studying biology, zoology, sociology

* His version of the original acoustic version of Dylan's song transcends the usual sense of the word 'cover'. Dylan now performs it the Hendrix way.

and botany. Far from being a distraction, his interest in different disciplines enriched and cross-pollinated his thinking. You can think of this as cultivating the mind: he would leave some fields of thought fallow to plough other pastures, and when he returned to the field he had left, he would find a fresh crop of connections growing. The farming analogy works well.

I've seen great talks about physics illuminated by parallel thinking from technology, and even cooking and fashion. I once saw a scientist who played the violin in between sections of his talk on the Large Hadron Collider to aid the audience's reflection.

Don't think you're deviating from the point by connecting your ideas with other disciplines. The spark you can create in your audience is often achieved by tangential, left-field thinking. Above all, bring in your own passions – whether these are fishing, playing the organ or the art of Raphael.

Hendrix expanded the minds of his listeners by challenging the narrow stereotype of what he should be playing, and of course *how* he should play it, even introducing sounds that were thought to be mistakes – like squally guitar feedback – into his numbers.

---

### Stay Fresh

A law of speaking is that whatever went well last time – a section, story or joke – will almost certainly not be a hit the next time round. It's no use thinking 'that was a winner with the previous audience – what's wrong with this lot?'

Staying fresh means always changing something – varying your start, using a different story, adding a new, experimental passage.

Great musicians will vary their playlist from night to night, thinking about this particular audience, venue or atmosphere, always searching for a perfect order for that night's occasion.

## Curiosity and creativity

Your passion as a speaker will be felt most keenly if you are relentlessly curious about what's new, stimulating and mind-stretching about your subject.

One way to achieve this is to take a leaf out of disc jockey John Peel's book. From the 1960s on, with psychedelia through punk, indie and many other on-the-edge genres, the BBC presenter was the pioneer of the new and the ground-breaking. He lost and gained numerous fans as he genuinely embraced novel sounds, usually before others were ready to hear them. Listening to Peel was a roller-coaster ride, and you always knew you were going to be challenged. His philosophy is encapsulated in an almost throwaway comment he made. He said that when faced with the choice of listening to something he'd already heard, or a new song, *he'd always choose to listen to the one he hadn't heard.*

How many of us can honestly say we'd do this as a reflex? Mostly we become set in our ways, our choices in music, theatre, literature, newspapers and many of our personal habits firmly established by the time we're in, say, our early thirties. Consequently, we may find ourselves stuck with the same materials, attitudes and examples in our speaking. As speakers, we are modelling our material. In other words, listeners will be affected by how we are, as much as by our content.

When we become stuck in our own thinking, it's hard to convey excitement and inspiration. Being passionate, like John Peel, about exploring new frontiers will also ignite the imagination of your listener.

New doesn't necessarily mean better: there's a lot of dross in so-called 'new' theories, as well as new music. But we won't find the gems, the pioneering examples and thinking, without being perpetually curious.

I've used this John Peel notion as an analogy for innovative thinking, which implies being open to the new, the 'nova'.

## Stay fresh

With music, it's clear that most people haven't listened to very many fresh and original sounds since they grew up. Not surprisingly, the common mindset is that 'there's been nothing decent recorded since 1963/1973/1983/1993' – delete according to your own age. Clearly, this is nonsense. While acknowledging the unforgettable power of a song that moved us in our impressionable youth, we think there's not much good stuff around – because we haven't *experienced* much new for years!

Of course, you have to search a bit. For most music aficionados it's obvious that the best songs are not in the charts. Search a little harder and you'll find that some of the finest music that's been written and performed is happening today. In rock, folk, classical or whatever genre. That's why Don McLean was wrong.

'American Pie' by McLean was a US number one in 1972. A very catchy number, but I object to the words 'the day the music died'. This refers to the 1959 death of the youthful Buddy Holly in an aeroplane crash. What? No Beatles, no folk revival, no indie, ambient, rock or even modern pop? Millions of people knew what George Harrison was talking about when he said, 'The Beatles saved the world from boredom.'

We don't know exactly what McLean intended, as he's often coy about what the lyrics mean. Except for his sharp reply in an interview: 'It means I never have to work again, if I don't want to.'*

A word you often hear about great artists or performers is that they are a 'genius'. It's a dangerous word to use, suggesting that you've either got it or you haven't, and that for most of us it's unattainable. 'Genius' isn't something that can be attained, like a promotion or the big house on the hill.

Consider the original meaning of genius: 'spirit attendant

* Alan Howard, *The Don McLean Story* (2007).

on a person'. You can think of this as your own spirit; only in relatively recent times have we assumed that genius is a gift granted to the few. While I don't advocate the overblown self-help literature that says anyone can become a Michelangelo or Steven Jobs, I do believe that staying curious is a way to enrich your own spirit, and that some of this will spill over positively into the way you talk to others.

Comedian Bill Hicks, normally irreverent, lauded Hendrix by saying he'd been deposited on Earth by aliens who said, 'OK, Jimi – see you back here in twenty-seven years. Show them how it's done.'

It wasn't really like that. Jimi paid his dues, and you have to do the same if you want to achieve mastery in speaking.

## Get Experienced: Things to think and do

◄◄ Reflect on who are the great thinkers, authors or sources of inspiration in your field. Go back to your roots and find something timeless and topically relevant in their approach.

▶ Find who you can apprentice yourself to, either live, or researching videos and transcripts of their talks. Practise sections of a talk in someone else's 'band', if you can: there's no substitute for trying it out live.

▶ Go to see a great speaker or musical performer. Focus on the *how* more than the *what*. Be geeky. Take notes.

▮▮ When faced with the choice of what source you should look at, do a John Peel and choose something left field, the one you wouldn't usually have picked. Think about how to apply this to other areas of life.

▮▮ Think of sections of your talk that you are bored with – or that the audience will find difficulty attending to. Consider how to make it come alive, be more direct or simply make it shorter.

▶ Spend time deliberately practising the aspects of your talk – or the way you deliver it – that you need to improve. Practise repeatedly the parts that don't convince YOU!

## Get Experienced: Your notes

# NINE

# THE ZEN OF PRESENTING

- ◆ Non-Violence – Your Attitude to the Audience
- ◆ Humility – Can You Be More Patient and Tolerant?
- ◆ The Breath of Inspiration
- ◆ Enjoy the Silence

Zen is the rock and roll – or even punk – of wise philosophies. Like music, it cuts through the rational to the emotional and beyond. Here I'm not literally talking about Zen practice, but hijacking it as a shorthand for thinking more profoundly about how you help your audience to connect with you and what you are saying. If Zen is ultimately about real humility and simplicity, then that's the spirit I'm invoking.

There's no 'things to do' prompts at the chapter end – these are ideas to help you think about presenting, and more than that, sense the effect you have on your listeners.

◆

## Non-Violence – Your Attitude to the Audience

In Buddhist thought, *ahimsa*, or non-violence, is a central precept.* What's this got to do with the art of speaking well? I mean, you aren't going to *attack* your listeners, are you?

The connection is more subtle than that. How you are – and how you feel about speaking – is going to reach your audience at a level where it's not heard, but felt. Fear or anxiety in you will be picked up, and while it's not literally violence you are spreading, it can violate or undermine your message. That's why it's important to have some regular practice like meditation that dissolves a lot of unnecessary anxiety and fear.

Nelson Mandela remarked: 'As we are liberated from our own fear, our presence automatically liberates others.'†

How you are affects the impact of your talk greatly, more than the subject matter or a clever technique. After all, your audience can probably find most of your content online. What people want is your personal take or spin, your enthusiasm and passion.

I was once taught something simple but transformative about teaching. When an audience member is aggressive, critical or negative, it's possible to get hooked into trying to win them over. In the past I've tried this and usually failed. I learned that it's just that person's own anxiety or anger coming out, and to see beyond their bluster to the person inside.

What I've taken from this simple observation is that no one can harm you in a talk, and therefore you don't need to attack back.

This doesn't mean lying down and limply agreeing with something you don't – that would be dumb – but is about *how* you deal with any objections. Above all, how you deal with the questioner. Taking every question and challenge absolutely seriously is the key to giving a satisfying answer.

* I'm not a Buddhist, though like many, I admire the benevolence of their world view.
† John Daido Loori, *The Zen of Creativity* (2005).

## Psychological judo

As a harmless way of dealing with aggressive questions, try the philosophy of judo – using the other's weight against them. Asking them to repeat their question or comment, more slowly and clearly this time, gradually begins to draw the sting out of it. Facetious questions are handled particularly well this way. Supreme patience can wear down even a bigot.

Before speaking to a new group, I've sometimes been briefed about who the difficult, loud-mouthed or troublesome attendees are likely to be. 'Watch out for Rolf – he likes to have a go at outside speakers.'

Almost inevitably I find out these are some of the most interesting people in the group, and sometimes we become friends. I don't have much feeling of fear or violence towards them, and they (usually) sense this and let me off the hook as a result.

Ahimsa doesn't mean being tolerant of everything. There's a saying that 'only dead fish go with the flow'. Let's think of the situation when someone comes up at the end of your talk, saying they want to give you some 'feedback'.

These people are not your friends. Firstly, you're probably not in a state of mind to receive feedback. Ask them to put it in writing, if they must.

Secondly, it almost certainly won't be useful. 'Feedback' should be neutral, but more often than not it's a put-down, and will feel like Hendrix's less pleasant experiments in sound rather than useful insight. 'Feed forward' is what you need, and I suggest this will be better heard later.

Smile nicely, and move away. Being humble doesn't mean being a pushover ...

## *Humility – Can You Be More Patient and Tolerant?*

Humility of spirit is a thread that runs through a lot of Zen teaching. There's a catch, though: as soon as you start describing yourself as humble, you're not. False modesty is easily sniffed out.

For the Dalai Lama, humility is connected to patience. In a high-velocity society, patience is one of the natural resources fast running out. 'The other queue always moves faster!' is a twenty-first-century koan that applies to most situations. Real patience is achieved when you can accept this in a way that means you've let go of your impatience.

In speaking, patience can be outwardly expressed by hearing out a questioner fully, giving attention as much to them as the content of what they are saying. It's harder to take questions on an equal footing if you are standing and they are sitting. There's a power imbalance, and this will probably be reflected in the kind of questions you receive.

Sit down, send the signal that this is collaborative now, and you have all the time in the world to hear their questions.


## Practical patience

Patience is a virtue. In part, it's based on not forgetting that you also were new to this topic once. You need to make the unreasonable (but useful) assumption that if they haven't 'got it', it's because you weren't clear enough explaining it. This is practical patience because it prompts you to try saying the same thing again, more slowly, or to find a fresh way of putting it.

One line not to use is, 'It's very simple.' The subtext behind this well-meaning phrase is that it *would* be simple, if you didn't have a brain the size of a pea!

### Cochran's Humility

Guitarist Eddie Cochran was a huge influence on sixties music with songs like 'Summertime Blues'. Asked what his biggest contribution to music was, he replied, 'Not singing.'

Sadly, he checked out in 1960, aged only twenty-one years.

Being humble doesn't mean being subservient, meek or fawningly obsequious in the way that waiters can be. It's not putting yourself above or below your students; neither arrogant, nor inferior.

Zen thinking is often paradoxical. While I believe I'm lucky to have worked with all these famous companies, I'm also confident enough to think (usually!) that they are lucky to have me. This mindset has helped me to be more patient and tolerant if a large organisation doesn't change as fast as I'd like, and it cuts both ways; customers tolerate more of my unusual approaches and eccentricities.

A humble relationship with your audience is built on the notion that it's a meeting of equals. The benefit of this was expressed nicely by Eleanor Roosevelt when she said, 'Nobody can make you feel inferior without your permission.' Instructed to be 'more humble', I'm not sure it's actionable. Break it down into patience and tolerance, and we've got something to work with.

There is one simple thing you can do to convey humility: admit you don't know when someone asks you a question. I often tell the group that the best questions are the ones that I *have no damned idea* how to answer.

Even better is to say, 'I have no idea – but you've made me determined to find out.' You're expressing the idea that this is an exchange with learning happening both ways. Again, it's mindset, not technique: you have to mean it.


## The Breath of Inspiration

There's pressure on talks today to be 'inspiring', but what does that really mean? *Spirare* is the Latin for breathe. Breath is essential not just to life, but also to the philosophy of Zen, where breathing in means taking in the whole universe, while breathing out is expelling it.

The creative and motivational stimulation that we call 'inspiration' has as much a physical as a metaphysical basis. It happens when the speaker's and the listener's breath are more in tune. Not figuratively, but literally.

Our mental state is supported by our physical state: if the body is breathing rapidly and our blood pressure is rising, we find it hard to be at peace and receptive to ideas. In contrast, ease in breathing equates to ease and openness of mind.

'Relax' is the single most useless instruction you can give or receive because the stress signals the body is sending out make it near impossible to respond. You may have been told, 'take deep breaths whenever you feel nervous'. It's unlikely to work – it's too late.

## Transcend

What does work is long-term practice of a technique like Transcendental Meditation (TM), which habituates the nervous system to breathe more easily, even when you're standing in front of an audience. That's why I've been practising and teaching it for over thirty years. Control of breath rarely works, but training your body to be relaxed while being active does.

How does this affect the audience? Mirror neurons is one of the exciting new areas of brain/ mind studies. These neurons fire in the same way when an animal acts – for instance, seizing a banana – as when it *merely observes* the same action performed by another. Shown in macaque monkeys, but not yet clearly enough in humans, the notion nevertheless makes sense; edging closer to a neuro-explanation of why you sometimes can feel a unity between you and others – your brains are firing as one.

Whether or not they eventually discover mirror neurons in the human brain, it's clear that for a speaker and audience to be in unison, there's a mirroring of breath patterns. You're energised? Then they will be. You're flat and uninspired yourself? Ditto. As mental states depend on the body's state, learn to breathe easier and so will the room.

In Zen thinking, there's an in-breath and an out-breath, for individuals and for the collective. Do you feel that wave of held breath, released together if you've surprised the group – or made them laugh? Be aware of that a little more and you will close the gap with your audience. Maybe not quite breathing as one, but definitely less separate.

The poet Rilke addresses breath as 'you invisible poem', describing it as a 'continual exchange of your existence'. Achieving continual exchange between you and your audience is what to go for, however it's described.

## Enjoy the Silence

'Everything comes out of nothing' is the apparently nonsensical view of many ancient philosophies. What it actually means is that the underlying state is a silent, inner consciousness that is *no-thing*: it can't be characterised or explained in everyday sensory terms because it lives beyond them. Silence is the basis of sound – it's the intervals between notes and silence that allow music and speech to become patterns that are recognised by our brains. Newton pointed out that it's not the waves of light that are coloured, but our brain's interpretation that makes it so. It's the same with speech and music.

Silence doesn't mean just quietness: it has a quality to it. The expectant hush before someone distinguished enters the room, or the mood of a group who seem uncomfortable with what you've just said. Both outwardly silent, both inwardly quite different.

I'm suggesting you not only allow more silences, pauses and moments of reflection between your own words, but that you also listen for the quality of the silence between you and others. Give it a name – like 'thoughtful', 'awkward', 'confused'. You'll soon learn to read it.

## Four minutes, thirty-three seconds of silence

John Cage is a famous and controversial composer touched by Zen. In 1952 he wrote what he was later to call his most important work – 4'33" – said as four minutes, thirty-three seconds. It's often called 4'33" of silence, but all the score tells the performers is *not* to play their instruments throughout its three movements. Cage's observation was that even in a non-echoing chamber, there is always sound, even if it's just that of your own blood circulating. In part he was responding to the visual artists who got there first: Rauschenberg had just painted the all-white canvasses he became well known for, and Cage wanted to do the same in music.

Many people's first response to the idea of 4'33" is that it's a silly joke, even an insult to an audience. Cage was a creative and incredibly penetrating thinker about music, and knew he'd get flak for the piece. I won't pretend to paraphrase his own motivation and philosophy here; his book on the topic is one I don't think I'll ever fully understand, couched as it is in Zen-ish ways that make you think, rather than giving you simple explanations.

4'33" captures the spirit of contrarian, creative thinking which I've been trying to express throughout *RYP*. What *can't* you do in a presentation? I hope my 'score' has been clear on the fact that you can do what you like, and if you have to start with doing the *opposite* of poor talks you've seen, it's a creative start. For example,

**'Tell them what you're going to tell them, and ...'**

Why? They'll die on you. Surprise, and gradually unveil.

**'Type your script out clearly, or have your notecards to hand.'**

Why? The listener wants to hear *you*, not your notes.

**'Avoid Death by PowerPoint.'**

How? Tell me about *life* with visuals, not the problems.

And so on ...

Frank Zappa did a great cover of 4'33" in a 1993 tribute to Cage. I like his version.

The other significant aspect of 4'33" is, of course, the silence itself. We've touched on this several times in *RYP*: the thought that too much noise (or too many words) gobbles up the $CO_2$ in the room, the fact that speech and music only exist because of different pitches or frequencies of sound against a backdrop of silence. In practice, this means pause, allow the silence and be sensitive to its different qualities.

## Creating a still centre

Stillness may be a more useful notion, if you find it hard to get your head around silence. Quiet Time* for students and teachers at the beginning and end of their school days is beginning to reduce the unnecessary stress or 'noise' in their environment, as well as ADHD. The still mind is more receptive and open: the over-busy one is so occupied playing its own inner 'music' of thoughts that it's hard to allow in the new.

So what can't you do when you've got too much material to get through? Why not do less. Cage-style, I have occasionally asked groups just to sit quietly for 4'33". After initial tittering and awkwardness, it's amazing the stillness that can settle over a room. It's not as profound as the one where people are actually meditating, but nonetheless it's a marked contrast to the jumpier atmosphere that's usually there. After a pause like this, a number of people have come up to me to say they rarely sat still for that long, and one or two remarked how they'd found greater clarity on a problem at work. Just by being still.

* Visit DavidLynchFoundation.org for inspiring videos on how Quiet Time is transforming schools.

You know what it's like when a crowd is touched by a mood of collective silence, in anticipation of some exciting event. Match point at Wimbledon, and the crowd will draw in their breath as one, sit perfectly still, and then let it out as one communal breath or eruption of life as the point is won and lost.

Wouldn't it be great if you could create that quality of attention in your talks? I believe that from time to time, you can. Stand perfectly still, collect yourself, gesture with your hands that this is a moment to settle down and listen in, then say something like, 'Listen to these words.' Pause. Say the important point, phrase or quote you want them to attend to. Repeat more slowly.

You'll notice that the fragmented thinking of the group funnels down to a point of stillness, of absorption in your point. It may not be quite like match point on Centre Court, and less effective with a class of hyperactive fourteen-year-olds, but usually you will have deepened the attention in the room.

I learned my own version of this from observing a brilliant speaker who is a master at commanding attention. She's commanding not just because of her words, but her ability to work with, allow and not be afraid of silences that helps her cast a spell over an audience.

The last words go to French art rockers Daft Punk, whose name has a whiff of Zen about it. Especially as they're not daft – reading their interviews demonstrates their depth of thought about the music they are creating – and they are certainly not playing punk. On their best-selling album, *Random Access Memories*, there's a surprisingly philosophical song called 'Beyond'. What they say can be applied equally to speaking and to music:

❝ The perfect song is framed with silence. ❞

# SLEEVE NOTES

## 1. Rock Your Presentation Events

I provide coaching to help you apply the ideas in *RYP* to a group's real presentation, or an actual pitch a team is working on. These events range from keynote speeches to longer intensive sessions,. The methods can also be applied to conference design, training and more learner-centred education.

The effect is to take people to the next level: we build on a basic knowledge of presenting, and use the philosophy that 'real is best' – actual presentations and real pitches are worked on, not theoretical ones.

There's no set outline here because events are all tailored. Though the core pieces of the jigsaw are the same – rocking up your content and delivery – they are put together in a unique way to fit the need.

Finally, I co-write important presentations, whether live or for video, and also do one-to-one coaching sessions.

For more information, or to book, email me at nigelbarlow@nigelbarlow.com. Or phone +44 (0)1865 512301. My website is www.nigelbarlow.com.

## 2. Other Speaking

Mainly I'm speaking, rather than talking about speaking. I talk about applied creativity and innovation, focused on, for example:

- Developing a culture of innovation
- Changing mindsets
- Creative leadership
- Rethinking: new challenges; new strategies
- Legendary customer experiences – in a time of digital transformation
- Inventing the future
- Fresh approaches to selling value

Facilitating, moderating and compering are roles I'm also asked to play, as well as creative event design and impactful communication materials and videos.

## 3. Recommended Books

On *presenting*, I recommend *Presentation Zen* by Garr Reynolds (New Riders, 2008). A great guide to the philosophy and practicalities of presenting in a clearer, more effective way.

On *pitching*, you'll find a great source book is *Perfect Pitch* by Jon Steel (Adweek Books, 2006). The last chapter on London's successful pitch to win the Olympics is worth the price of the book.

On *language*, I've raved about Mark Forsyth's *The Elements of Eloquence* (Icon Books, 2013). Anything by him is a delight, and a real shot in the arm for the language lover. If even a tiny bit rubs off on you, it will be reflected in more interesting use of language.

On *music* you will find a lot to think about in Daniel Levitin's *This Is Your Brain on Music* (Atlantic Books, May 2006). A former musician who became a neuroscientist at McGill University, Levitin explains our fascination with music, and what we now know about its impact on the brain.

Then there's *How Music Works* by David Byrne (Canongate Books, 2012). The former Talking Heads front man talks about the environment and technologies that shaped music, and has a better vocabulary – and understanding – than most musical journalists.

Finally, do try *Instrumental* by James Rhodes (Canongate Books, 2015). It's a very powerful read – music literally saved his life. It's rare to read such personal honesty, interwoven with his observations on the restorative power of music. He's now a concert pianist, intent on shaking up the stuffiness of the classical music world. Not by watering down or any cross-over with pop, but by deepening the intensity with which audiences experience the work.


## 4. New Sounds

Do you feel as if your taste is stuck in the past and you need a reboot? Ask friends for recommendations, and if you're feeling bolder, even ask the kids!

The best sounds are almost certainly not in the charts, so here are some pointers if you're keen to discover something new. Look for off-centre labels – you can find a whole world of great stuff just by exploring the *Secretly Canadian* catalogue.

Dip into the music sections of papers. For intelligent reviews, it's hard to beat the *FT's Weekend Life and Art* section, or the music reviews in Friday's *Guardian*. Some of the music magazines include a CD (or, increasingly, downloads of new music): you can find some real winners here.

Then, of course, there's all the streaming services – Apple music, Spotify, Tidal and Last.fm and enthusiasts' sites like Pitchfork. Don't know where to begin? They have playlists for you to sample with headings like Chill, Alternative, Dance or whatever. Listen to one of these, dive further into an artist who appeals to you, and that could be your evening gone.

The second-best source of new sounds is passionate recommendations. But there's a caveat. People's musical tastes are so varied and unpredictable – we all see different faces when we look in the fire – that when someone is too persuasive about why you *should* like this it can put you off.

The best source is your own curiosity. That's why I'm not going to recommend anything. Except to say that if you haven't heard Natalie Merchant, Lucinda Williams, Richard Thompson, Magnolia Electric Company, Tricky, Amadou and Mariam, The Shins, Stephen Duffy, Rodrigo y Gabriela, Frank Turner, Alela Diane, Land of Talk, Arthur Russell, Beach House, Rilo Kiley and a thousand others, then you've missed some great stuff.

Mostly I have a passion for the unknown, the underrated or the outsider. Nick Harper is someone who fits the bill here – without doubt the finest combination of lyrics, voice and guitar performing in the UK today. Find one of his concerts – on harperspace.com – and go and say 'hi' to Nick. His passion and intensity is a live demonstration of much of what I've written in *Rock Your Presentation*.

Go to my website, www.nigelbarlow.com, and you'll find links to download much of the music mentioned in *RYP*, as well as some new stuff to try.

## 5. Calm Energy

When I'm asked where I get my energy from, I'm not sure if people believe me, unless they've tried it. I'm talking about my daily practice of Transcendental Meditation, or TM. Strange name, highly effective technique, and it's the one with the greatest volume and quality of scientific research behind it.

You do it for fifteen to twenty minutes twice daily, eyes closed, sitting in a comfortable chair, at home or on a train or plane – it's very portable. TM's not a religion, philosophy or way of life, but an effortless and enjoyable method for allowing mind and body to transcend – or go beyond – agitation and stress. You settle into a wonderful and unique state of calm, and when you open your eyes you take some of this restful alertness into your life: you think more clearly and creatively, react faster and it's much more difficult to be phased. Stress comes and goes, but it doesn't leave such a big impression on your nervous system – and your nerves.

You have to learn from a trained teacher – don't go for some-one who has just done a bit of yoga and read up on it because it won't work. TM teachers undergo years of training, and teach the precise, but easy-to-learn technique in a systematic way around the world.

This is one of the few areas of life where I'd urge you to only go with the official organisation, or you'll learn a less effective version. In the UK the contact details are Uk.tm.org. Tel.+44 (0)1695 51213. They can also put you in touch with the official teaching organisation in your country.

I am very proud to be a trustee of the UK David Lynch Foundation, a registered charity which teaches TM to the world's most at risk populations – from street kids in Brazil and Colombia to abused women in Africa, children and teach-ers in thousands of schools in North and South America, to service men and women with PTSD. As I've talked in *RYP* about sharing your passions, this is one that's very dear to my heart – go to davidlynchfoundation.org, and if you're not moved at least a little by the stories of change from within I'd be surprised.

All of us get stressed, and this is the most effective way ordinary people like me and you can learn to manage it better, without any need for mind games, control or effort. I'm sure I wouldn't have had the guts – or the energy – to stand in front of a hall full of people and feel (mostly) at ease, if it wasn't for the cumulative effects of many years of TM.

# ACKNOWLEDGEMENTS

Firstly, I'd like to thank my clients around the world – many of whom have become friends – for hiring me to do what I love doing. Without the opportunities they've given me, I wouldn't have been able to write this book from the point of view of experience.

Then there are my close friends and colleagues – Matt Dickinson, Robert Maguire, Alison Weller and Ian Taylor. Brian Weller has also been a great source of inspiration, and has given generous help well beyond the expected in many long distance calls to California.

Richard Shakespeare of IBM and Neil Jordan of Microsoft – both passionate about music – deserve a huge thank you for checking the accuracy of musical concepts. You probably didn't know what you were in for when you agreed to this, but I'm indebted for your care and perseverance. My literary agent Robert Dudley has been a tower of good humour and common sense, and at Little, Brown Meri Pentikäinen has been wonderfully encouraging and supportive.

Journalist, film-maker and friend Josh Freed made a number of useful and insightful comments. Also, I'm grateful to Hyman Weisbord, Merrilly Weisbord and Kathleen McDonald for letting me write and think in their lovely wood in Canada.

My family can't be thanked enough. Especially Angie, for her love, creative insight and constant encouragement. And my wonderful musical children, Jamie and Rosie.

The biggest debt of all is to Janet Hanson, who has cajoled, motivated and guided me throughout, doing everything from the practicalities of formatting the book to giving perceptive advice on its content, voice and logic. Thanks, Jan – no way could I have done this without you.

# INDEX

(page numbers in *italic* type refer to illustrations)

**A**
ad libs, rehearsing 60
Adams, Henry 194
Adams, Ryan 124
Adele 88
'Albatross' 88
'All Along the Watchtower' 213
*All We Are Saying* (Sheff) 40*n*
Allen, Woody 189
'Am I Wry? No!' 92
'American Pie' 216
Andreesen, Marc 89
'Anthem' 151
Apple 51–2, 81
Apple Education 22
audience:
   and breakout sessions 170–4
      capturing voices 172–4, *172*, *173*
      creative 171–2
   engagement with 158–79 (*see also*
      performance; presentation)
      call and response 166–8
      and 'duets' 168–9
      gospel style 166–9
      spectrum describing *159*–60
      summarised 178
   gap between speaker and 62–3, *63*
   inviting on stage 174
   and panels 175–7
      making it conversational 176–7
   and Q&A sessions 160–6
      and perception gap 162
      and Socratic method 164
      and thoughtful questions 165–6
      types of question 164
   researching 60–5
      and ignoring 62
Ayers, Kevin 146

**B**
'Badge' 208
Baez, Joan 41–2
Baker, Ginger 176
Ballmer, Steve 133
Band 48
Barclays 32
'In The Battle of Sun vs Curtains, Sun
      Loses and We Sleep Until Noon' 92
Beach House 27
Beatles 38–9, 92, 210
Beethoven, Ludwig 7
Belle and Sebastian 85
*The Better Angels of Our Nature* (Pinker)
    94
'Beyond' 229
'Billie Jean' 106
BlackBerry 89
Blair, Tony 84
*Blink* (Gladwell) 76*n*
*Blood Money* 83
*Bloom* 27
'Bohemian Rhapsody' 91–2
Bolan, Marc 181
Bono 161
books, recommended 231–2
'Born to Run' 27
Bowie, David 27, 37, 48, 181–2
   cut-up method of 66–7
Boyd, Joe 207*n*
Brecht, Bertolt 152
Brown, James 133
Brown, Thom 122
Brozman, Bob 105
Buffett, Warren 89
Burroughs, William 66
Buzan, Tony 205–6
Byrne, David 20

## C

Cage, John 227–8
Callas, Maria 155
'Can't Buy Me Love' 25
Carey, Mariah 151
Carnegie, Andrew 32
*Carrie & Lowell* 21
Cash, Johnny 148–9
'Changes' 27
Chekhov, Anton 79
Churchill, Winston 60, 163
Cirque du Soleil 204
Civil Wars 106
Clapton, Eric 62
Cobain, Kurt 124, 181
Cochran, Eddie 223
Cochran, Johnnie 26
Cohen, Adam 79
Cohen, Leonard 79, 132, 151
'Collaboration Don't Work' 32n
Collins, Albert 202
Columbo (character) 197
core strengths 49
Coyle, Daniel 211
'Crazy Water' 150
Cream 176, 208
Crosby, Bing 142
Crow, Sheryl 148

## D

Daft Punk 229
Dalai Lama 223
Darwin, Charles 213–14
Davies, Ray 137
de Luca, Gabriel 138
Descartes, René 148
Diamond, Bob 32
'Diamonds and Rust' 42
Diana, Princess of Wales 84
Dickinson, Bruce 120–1
Dickinson, Matt 28–9, *63*, 108
*The Don McLean Story* (Howard) 216n
Drake, Nick 82, 105, 124
Drucker, Peter 58–9
Dubner, Stephen J. 91
Dylan, Bob 36, 48, 65–6, 155, 209, 213

## E

Edison, Thomas 192
Einstein, Albert 16, 88
Elbow 151
'Eleanor Rigby' 25, 92
*The Elements of Eloquence* (Forsyth) 83–4
Elsbach, Kimberly 188
Eminem 41
Eno, Brian 212
Evans, Paul 'Chubby' 116
events 230
Everything but the Girl 136

## F

Fairport Convention 207
Faithfull, Marianne 152
*Faking It* (Barker, Taylor) 86
FedEx 78
*Feral* (Monbiot) 94n
*Fermat's Last Theorem* (Singh) 78
FFS 32
*Firm Commitment* (Mayer) 32
Fleetwood Mac 88
format and structure 15–46 (*see also* power-chord techniques)
  as 'album' 36
  brevity of 16–19
  bridge/middle eight 27–31, 102
    and minor keys and emotions 30–1
    as side story 28–9
  climax of: codas and fades 31–2
    and leaving audience on a high 33–5
    rising to 32
  coherence of 37–8
  conclusion of, and leaving audience on a high 33–5
  and 'greatest hits' talk, avoiding 37
  opening bars of 19–23
    as provocation 21–3
    silence in 20–1
  and 'psycho-logic' 38–40
  simplicity of 36–7
  summarised 44
  three-act structure of 40–1
  verse and chorus 23–7
    breaking rules of 25
    and call and response 25–7
    and the 'so what?' chorus 24–5
Forsyth, Mark 83–4
4'33" 227–8
Franklin, Aretha 169
Frayn, Michael 18–19
*Freakonomics* (Levitt, Dubner) 91, 94
Future Islands 144

## G

Gallo, Carmine 10
Gandhi, Mohandas (Mahatma) 87
Garvey, Guy 151
Gassée, Jean-Louis 187
Gates, Bill 210
Gawande, Dr Atul 73–4
Genzlinger, Neil 17
Gettysburg Address 15
Ghost 92
Gibran, Kahlil 151
Gladwell, Malcolm 76–7, 210n, 213
Glastonbury Festival 53
Gore, Al 122
Green, Philip 113

**H**

'Happy' 88
'Happy Jack' 81
'Hard to Love a Man' 169*n*
Harper, Nick 233
Harrison, George 216
'Heartbreak Hotel' 141
Hendrix, Jimi 201–2, 205, 207, 210, 212–13, 214, 217, 222
Herring, Samuel T. 144
Heward, Lyn 204
Hewlett Packard 122
Hicks, Bill 217
*High Fidelity* (Hornby) 10
Holiday, Billie 147, 148
Holly, Buddy 216
Hornby, Nick 10
Horton, Matthew 27–8
Howard, Alan 216*n*
Howlin' Wolf 71
'Hurt' 148–9


**I**

'I Am the Walrus' 92
I Love You … But I've Chosen Darkness 92
'I Still Believe' 177
'Immigrant Song' 19
Imposter Syndrome 4–5, 154–5
*An Inconvenient Truth* 122
*Information Is Beautiful* (McCandless) 120
*In Search of Excellence* (Peters) 104, 206
*Instrumental* (Rhodes) 7*n*, 184
iPhone 89


**J**

Jackson, Michael 106
Jobs, Steve 185, 210
    on creativity 3
    and micromanagement 51–2
    and presentation 10
'Johnny Delusional' 32
Johnson, Steven 77
Johnson, Willy 71
Jones, Norah 151
Julien, Olivier 39*n*
Jung, Carl 93
Jurado, Damien 169*n*


**K**

Keynote and PowerPoint, *see* presentation: with slides and visuals
King, Martin Luther 147, 166
Kings of Convenience 92
Kinks 71, 137
KLF 148
Knight, Curtis 205
Kooper, Al 65–6
Kramer, Roderick 188


**L**

Larson, Gary 36
Lasseter, John 185
'The Laughing Gnome' 48
Led Zeppelin 19
Lee, Stewart 94
Lehman Brothers 32
Lennox, Annie 169
Levitt, Steven D. 91
LIBOR scandal 32
'Like a Rolling Stone' 65–6
'Little Green' 77
'Little Lou, Ugly Jack, Prophet John' 85
Little Richard 205
Loori, John Daido 203, 221*n*
Lopez, Jennifer 50
'A Love that Burns' 105
*Low* 37, 182
Lowe, Nick 85
'Lucy in the Sky with Diamonds' 92


**M**

McCandless, David 120
McCartney, Paul 25
McCormack, Mark 90
McDonald, Ian 82–3
McLean, Don 216
Madonna 132
Magnolia Electric Company 169*n*
Maguire, Robert 25–6, 123, 173*n*
Mandela, Nelson 221
'Mannish Boy' 105
Marley, Bob 35
Maslow, Abraham 32
Mayer, Colin 32
Melua, Katie 93
Mew 92
micromanagement 51–2
Microsoft 133
'Miss You' 208
Mitchell, Joni 30, 77
Monbiot, George 94
'Money' 175
Moore, Alan F. 39*n*
'My Generation' 71, 81
'My Old Man' 30


**N**

Nasrudin, Mulla 75–6
Nelson, Horatio 29
*Never Mind the Bollocks* 103
*New York Times* 17
Newton, Isaac 226
*The Next Day* 27*n*
9/11 95
Nine Inch Nails 149
Nine Million Bicycles (in Beijing) 93
Nirvana 71, 124

**O**
Obama, Barack 85
Orton, Beth 152–3
*Outliers* (Gladwell) 210*n*

**P**
'Paranoid Android' 32
Partytecture 116
Pascale, Richard 74–5
PayPal 18
PechaKucha, *see* presentation: with slides and visuals
Peel, John 215
*The People's Music* (McDonald) 82*n*
performance 131–57 (*see also* audience; presentation)
  and body language 140–5
    being animated 143–5
    expression 144
  doing protest 147–8
  with imperfections 151–5
    by being yourself 152–3
    and riskiness 154–5
    without self-erasing 153–4
  with passion 144, 145–51
    and enthusiasm 150–1
    and intimate thoughts 148–50
    making it personal 146–7
  and presence 134–40
    by breaking 'fourth wall' 137–8
    and eye positions and movements 138
    the here and now of 135–6
    and scripts and notes 138–9
    'switching channels' 136
    summarised 156
  warming up for 132–4
    and your entrance 133–4
Peters, Tom 104, 137, 206
Picasso, Pablo 52, 210
'Pictures of Lily' 81
Pink Floyd 175
Pinker, Steven 95
Pinker, Susan 26*n*
pitching:
  'opening bars' of 22, 183–5
  preparation for 59
  vs presentation 8–9, *9*
  with slides and visuals 118–19
  top ten tips for 180–98
    demonstrating 192–4
    dressing 186–7
    fewer words and slides 197–8
    getting into people's heads 181–3
    keeping it real ('unplugged') 190–1
    less time 198, *198*
    making people care 183–5
    questioning 194–7
    starting a conversation 187–90

  thinking beyond 185–6
Pixar 185
*Planes, Trains, and Automobiles* 73
Power, Cat 24
power-chord techniques 71–98 (*see also* structure and format)
  and great lyrics 83–90
    alliteration in 84
    avoiding clichés in 86–7
    from choice reading 85–6
    golden facts in 93–6
    names in 92–3
    quotations in 88–90
    with strong titles 90–3
    thinking beyond obvious 86
    tricolons in 85
  stories 72–8
    backstory 77–8
    teaching 74–7
  summarised 97
  word pictures 78–83
    appealing to senses 81–3
*The Power of Positive Deviance* (Pascale, Sternin, Sternin) 74–5
PowerPoint and Keynote, *see* presentation: with slides and visuals
presentation (*see also* audience; performance):
  and calm energy 233
  lo-fi ('unplugged') 124–8
    and going acoustic 126–8
    and technology meltdown 124–6
  and microphones 56, 57, 103, 104
  with passion 145–51
    making it personal 146–7
  vs pitching 8–9, *9*
  and props 120–3
    simple 120–3
    yourself as 123
  sound and vision of 101–30
    summarised 129
  and speaking:
    'apprenticeship' 205–12
    creative copying 202
    curiosity and creativity 214
    deliberate practice 211–12
    expanding the mind 212–17
    inspiration 213–14
    learning from masters 201–19
    observing and learning 206–7
    originality 204–5
    putting in the time 210–11
    staying fresh 214, 216
    summarised 218
  using slides and other visuals, *see* slides and visuals
  on video 56–7
  and vocal delivery, *see* voice
  Zen of 220–9
    creating a still centre 228–9

enjoying silence 226–30
humility 222–4
inspiration 224–6
non-violence 221–2
psychological judo 222
transcending 225–6
*The Presentation Secrets of Steve Jobs* (Gallo) 10
*Presentation Zen* (Reynolds) 119
Presley, Elvis 27, 141–2
Prezi, *see* presentation: with slides and visuals
*The Prophet* (Gibran) 151*n*
'Psycho Killer' 20

### Q
Quakers 32
Queen 91–2
*Quiet Is the New Loud* 92

### R
Radiohead 32
*Raiders of the Lost Arc* 19
Raitt, Bonnie 207
*Random Access Memories* 229
Rankin, Bill 22–3
Red Hot Chili Peppers 148
'Red House' 202
Reith, John 73
Reith Lectures 73
*Rethink – How to Think Differently* (Barlow) 78*n*
Reynolds, Garr 119
Rhodes, James 7, 184
Richards, Keith 53
riders:
    personal 47–9
        and core strength 49
    technical 50–2
        and micromanagement 51–2
Rilke, Rainer Maria 226
'River Man' 82
Roddick, Anita 72
'Rollin' in the Deep' 88
Rolling Stones 24, 53, 143, 205, 208
Rubin, Rick 148–9
Rutherford, Lord 80

### S
'Satisfaction' 24
Sculley, John 185
*Sgt. Pepper's Lonely Hearts Club Band* 38–9
setting the stage 46–70
    lighting 57
    and personal rider 47–9
        and core strength 49
    rehearsals 58–60
        of ad libs 60

researching audience 60–5 (*see also* audience)
    gap between speaker and 62–3, *63*
    and ignoring 62
    site visit as part of 52–6
    and preparing the room 54–5
    sound check 56–7
    summarised 69
    and technical rider 50–2
        and micromanagement 51–2
    watching other speakers 57–8
    and your first 'take' 65–8
Sex Pistols 103
*Sgt. Pepper and the Beatles* (Julien) 39*n*
Shakespeare, William 84, 103–4
Sheeran, Ed 148
Sheff, David 40*n*
Simpson, O. J. 26
Simpson, Robert 118
Singh, Simon 78
'Sisters Are Doing It for Themselves' 169
Slayer 148
slides 16–17
slides and visuals 109–20, 197–8, *197*
    going beyond bullet points 117
    image sources 117
    less is more 111–12
    mental interaction 112–14
    top ten principles 115–16
Smith, Fred 78
Socrates 164
'Sound and Vision' 37
Sparks 32
Springsteen, Bruce 27
'Stagefright' 48
'Stan' 41
'The Star-Spangled Banner' 213
Starr, Ringo 38–9
Sternin, Jerry 74–5
Sternin, Monique 74–5
Stevens, Sufjan 21
Stevenson, Jake 52, 56
Stills, Stephen 17
*Stop Making Sense* 20
stories 72–8
    backstory 77–8
    teaching 74–7
'Strange Fruit' 147
'Strawberry Fields Forever' 92
structure and format 15–46 (*see also* power-chord techniques)
    as 'album' 36
    brevity of 16–19
    bridge/middle eight 27–31, 102
        and minor keys and emotions 30–1
        as side story 28–9
    climax of: codas and fades 31–2
        and leaving audience on a high 33–5
        rising to 32
    coherence of 37–8

structure and format – *continued*
  conclusion of, and leaving audience on
    a high 33–5
  and 'greatest hits' talk, avoiding 37
  opening bars of 19–23
    as provocation 21–3
    silence in 20–1
  and 'psycho-logic' 38–40
  simplicity of 36–7
  summarised 44
  three-act structure of 40–1
  verse and chorus 23–7
    breaking rules of 25
    and call and response 25–7
    and the 'so what?' chorus 24–5
'Substitute' 81
summaries:
  audience, engagement with 178
  format and structure 44
  performance 156
  power-chord techniques 97
  presentation:
    sound and vision of 129
    and speaking 218
  setting the stage 69
  structure and format 44
*Superfreakonomics* (Levitt, Dubner) 91
'Suspicious Minds' 27

**T**

*The Talent Code* (Coyle) 211*n*
*Talk Like TED* (Gallo) 10
Talking Heads 20
Taylor, Ian 135–6
*Thelma and Louise* 40, 41
Theremin, Leon 120–1
Thiel, Peter 18
Thompson, Richard 207–9
Thorn, Tracey 136
'Toad' 176
Tomlin, Lily 88
Transcendental Meditation. 132, 225,
  233–4
Tricky 174
Troggs 213
Turner, Frank 158–9, 160, 177
Turner, Ike 205
Twain, Mark 163
Twitter 18

**U**

U2 148

**V**

Van Halen, Eddie 50
video presentations 56–7
*The Village Effect* (Pinker) 26*n*
Visconti, Tony 181–2
voice 102–9
  clarity of 107
  tempo of 104–7
  tone of 108–9
  volume of 103–4
'Voodoo Chile' 202

**W**

Waits, Tom 83
Was (Not Was) 150
*Watching the Dark* 209
Waters, Muddy 105, 202, 205
*Week* 88*n*
Weill, Kurt 152
Weller, Alison 138
Weller, Brian 38, 104
'For What It's Worth' 17
*What They Don't Teach You at Harvard
  Business School* (McCormack) 90
'What Were the Chances' 169*n*
'What's So Funny 'Bout Peace and Love
  and Understanding?' 85
*Where Good Ideas Come From* (Johnson) 77
Who 71, 81
Whyte, David 63–4
'Wild Thing' 213
Williams, Lucinda 151
Williams, Pharrell 88
Wodehouse, P. G. 187
Wood, Ronnie 143
Woodpigeon 92

**Y**

'You Really Got Me' 71
Young, Neil 151

**Z**

*Zelig* 189
*The Zen of Creativity* (Loori) 203, 221*n*
Zola, Émile 143